A BRIEF ETERNITY

*To the memory of my professor, Vladimir Jankélévitch,
so eloquent, so elegant.*

PASCAL BRUCKNER

A Brief Eternity

A Philosophy of Longevity

Translated by Steven Rendall and Lisa Neal

polity

Originally published in French as *Une brève éternité: Philosophie de la longévité* © Editions Grasset & Fasquelle, 2019

This English edition © Polity Press, 2021

Polity Press
65 Bridge Street
Cambridge CB2 1UR, UK

Polity Press
101 Station Landing
Suite 300
Medford, MA 02155, USA

ISBN-13: 978-1-5095-4432-5

A catalogue record for this book is available from the British Library.

Library of Congress Cataloging-in-Publication Data
Names: Bruckner, Pascal, author. | Rendall, Steven, translator. | Neal, Lisa (Lisa Dow), translator.
Title: A brief eternity : a philosophy of longevity / Pascal Bruckner ; translated by Steven Rendall and Lisa Neal.
Other titles: Brève éternité. English
Description: Cambridge ; Medford, MA : Polity, [2020] | "Originally published in French as Une brève éternité. Philosophie de la longévité © Editions Grasset & Fasquelle, 2019." | Includes bibliographical references. | Summary: "A brilliant philosophical reflection on the meaning of life after 50"-- Provided by publisher.
Identifiers: LCCN 2020023219 (print) | LCCN 2020023220 (ebook) | ISBN 9781509544325 (hardback) | ISBN 9781509544349 (epub)
Subjects: LCSH: Older people--Conduct of life. | Longevity--Philosophy. | Longevity--Social aspects.
Classification: LCC BJ1691 .B8513 2020 (print) | LCC BJ1691 (ebook) | DDC 128--dc23
LC record available at https://lccn.loc.gov/2020023219
LC ebook record available at https://lccn.loc.gov/2020023220

Typeset in 11 on 13pt Sabon
by Fakenham Prepress Solutions, Fakenham, Norfolk NR21 8NL
Printed and bound in Great Britain by CPI Group (UK) Ltd, Croydon

The publisher has used its best endeavours to ensure that the URLs for external websites referred to in this book are correct and active at the time of going to press. However, the publisher has no responsibility for the websites and can make no guarantee that a site will remain live or that the content is or will remain appropriate.

Every effort has been made to trace all copyright holders, but if any have been overlooked the publisher will be pleased to include any necessary credits in any subsequent reprint or edition.

For further information on Polity, visit our website:
politybooks.com

Contents

Contents

Part III
Late Love Affairs

Part IV
Fulfill Oneself or Forget Oneself?

Part V
What Does Not Die in Us

A bad life is more to be feared than death.

BERTOLT BRECHT

A Note on the Text

Chapter 10, "The Immortality of Mortals," was taken from a talk given at the French Embassy in New York in November 2014, as part of a series of seminars organized by the Onassis Foundation.

Part I, "The Indian Summer of Life," was published in no. 202 of the journal *Le Débat* in November 2018.

Here I explore in greater depth a reflection begun in *La Tentation de l'innocence* (1995; *The Temptation of Innocence*, 2000) and continued in *L'Euphorie perpétuelle* (2000; *Perpetual Euphoria*, 2010), *Le Paradoxe amoureux* (2009; *The Paradox of Love*, 2012) and *Le Mariage d'amour a-t-il échoué?* (2010; *Has Marriage for Love Failed?*, 2013), on the theme of beginning over, of unceasing resumption. Many echoes of these works will be found in this one.

The Unfrocked Priests of the Cult of Youth

In his autobiographical book *The World of Yesterday* (1942), Stefan Zweig tells how, in the Vienna of the late nineteenth century, in the Austro-Hungarian Empire, ruled by a seventy-year-old sovereign surrounded by tremulous courtiers, public opinion held young people in suspicion. Woe to anyone who retained a boyish appearance: he would not find a job, and the appointment of Gustav Mahler at the age of thirty-seven as the director of the Court Opera was a scandalous exception. Being young was then a hindrance in all careers. Ambitious men had to look more aged, begin to get old when they were still adolescents, encouraging their beards by shaving every day, putting gold-rimmed spectacles on their noses, wearing starched collars, stuffing themselves into rigid clothes, forcing themselves to don a long black tailcoat and, if possible, to display a little plumpness as a sign of being a serious person. Putting on the vestments of old age when one was only twenty was the condition *sine qua non* of success. It was necessary to punish the coming generations, which were already penalized by a humiliating, mechanical education, to tear them away from their first faltering

1

attempts, their scampish lack of discipline. A victory of the gravity that the honorable age has established as the only civilized behavior of humanity.

What a contrast with our own time, when any adult seeks desperately to display the outward signs of juvenility, wears unconventional clothes, long hair or jeans, when even mothers dress as their daughters do to erase any gap between them. In the old days, people lived the life of their ancestors, generation after generation. Now ancestors want to live the life of their descendants. People are *adulescens* at the age of forty, then *quincados, sexygenarians*, adventurers at seventy and more; with backpacks, ski poles in their hands and protective helmets on their heads, experts at Nordic walking go out to cross the street or public parks as if they were attacking Mount Everest or the Kalahari Desert, grandmothers on scooters, grand-dads on roller-skates or unicycles. A vertiginous authorized regression. The generational discord is as comic as it is symptomatic: between the young dandies crammed into suits like corsets and old children with silvery temples walking around in shorts, chronology is turned topsy-turvy.

In the meantime, values have been inverted: for Plato, the order of kinds of knowledge was supposed to follow that of ages: only someone over fifty could contemplate the Good. The leadership of his Republic was supposed to be reserved, by a sort of "tempered gerontocracy,"[1] only for the elders, who were capable of preventing the anarchy of passions and guiding citizens toward a high degree of humanity. The exercise of power was connected with spiritual authority. It was Plato, long before F. Scott Fitzgerald's *Benjamin Button*, who imagined, in his *Statesman*, that in olden days "dead elders emerged from the earth to live their lives in reverse," returning to the state of newborns. Thus childhood was seen as the end of existence, a return to the point of departure after a long journey. The beginning was an end and the end was a beginning.

We have developed a different view regarding this subject: for a century, ever since the catastrophe of World War I, which saw a whole age group vanish under the command of irresponsible generals, it has been maturity that is perceived as a fall, as if maturing was always dying a little bit.[2] The abominable thing about war is that it reverses priorities and makes sons die before their fathers. It is then that the young become, with surrealism and May '68, Rimbaud's heirs, the reservoir of all promises, the very crystallization of human genius. "Never trust anyone over 30," the American agitator and pacifist Jerry Rubin said in the 1960s, before he, too, became a prosperous businessman after turning forty. From this inversion arose a new attitude: the cult of youth, a symptom of ageing societies, the ideology of adults who want to combine all the benefits and the irresponsibility of childhood with the autonomy of adults. The cult of youth is destroyed even as it asserts itself: every day, those who sing its praises lose a little more the right to appeal to it, because they are getting old in turn. They transform an ephemeral privilege into a permanent title of nobility. The demolishers of one period become the outmoded of the next. The member of the avant-garde becomes an early candidate for the title of fuddy-duddy, the senile young man is transformed into a pensioner living off his senility. Even the baby-boomers, those fanatics of adolescence, end up becoming septuagenarians or octogenarians. The society of the youth cult is peculiar in that, far from being the triumph of hedonism, it is, from early childhood on, obsessed with senescence and tries to eliminate it through preventive over-medicalization. And its counterfeit eternal youth rings increasingly false as time goes on.

Up to the age of thirty, the human animal has no age, just eternity in front of it. For it, birthdays are amusing formalities, inoffensive scansions. Then come the multiples of ten, the list of decades – thirties, forties, fifties. Getting old is first of all just that: being put under house arrest in the calendar, becoming the contemporary of past periods. Age humanizes time but also makes it more dramatic. The sadness of toeing the line, having the common condition catch up with you. I have a certain age, but I'm not necessarily that age, I register a discrepancy between the representations associated with vital statistics and what I feel. When this discrepancy becomes massive, as it is right now, when in 2019 a Dutch citizen of sixty-nine files a complaint against the state because he feels that he is inwardly only forty-nine and suffers from discriminations at work and in his romantic life, we are witnessing a shift in mentalities. For the better and for the worse. People insist on living several times, in their own way. We no longer look our age because age has ceased to make us or break us: it's just one variable among others. We no longer want to be permanently attached to our birthdate, our sex, our skin color, our status: men want to be women and vice versa, or neither one nor the other; whites think they're black, old men think they're kids, adolescents falsify their ages in order to drink alcohol or get into a disco; the human condition is leaking on all sides – we are entering into the era of liquid generations and ideas. We no longer want to yield to the intimidation of big numbers; we demand the right to move the cursor the way we want to. Recently naturalized in the tribe of quadragenarians or sexagenarians, we begin by rejecting its codes. Age is a convention to which everyone adapts with greater or lesser grace. It pigeonholes us in roles and postures that the development of the sciences and the prolongation of life make obsolete. Today, many people want to escape this straitjacket and take advantage of the moratorium between maturity and old age to reinvent a new art of living. In what might be called the "Indian summer" of life, the baby-boomers are in this respect pioneers; they created the road they are traveling. They invented youth, and now they think they are reinventing old age. People remain hale and hearty so long as their psychological age doesn't coincide with their biological and social age. Nature may be our master, but it is less than ever our guide. We move forward resisting its ukases, because it constructs us only by destroying us, with majestic indifference.

An intellectual autobiography as much as it is a manifesto, this book deals with one question only: the length of life. It focuses on middle age, beyond fifty, when we are neither young nor old but still have an abundance of appetites. In this interval all the great questions of the human condition arise: do we want to live a long time or intensely, to continue along the same path or go off in another direction? What about remarrying, or starting a new career? How can we avoid the weariness of living, the melancholy of the twilight years? How can we get through great joys and great pains? What is the strength that keeps us afloat despite bitterness or satiety? These pages are dedicated to all those who dream of a new spring in the autumn of life and want to put off winter as long as they can.

PART I

The Indian Summer of Life

CHAPTER 1

Giving Up on Giving Up

Growing old is the only way we've found to live a long time.

SAINTE-BEUVE

What has changed in our societies since 1945? This funda-mental fact: life has ceased to be short, as ephemeral as a passing train, to borrow a metaphor from Maupassant. Or, rather, it is simultaneously too short and too long, oscillating between the burden of *ennui* and the glitter of urgency. It stretches into endless periods or flashes by like a dream. For the past century, the human species has been prolonging things, at least in rich countries, where life expectancy has increased by twenty to thirty years. Destiny has granted a leave, varying in length depending on sex and social class, to everyone. Medicine, "that armed form of our finitude," as Michel Foucault called it, accords us an additional generation – an immense advance, because this desire to live fully is accompanied by a recession of the threshold of old age, which began, two centuries ago, at the age of thirty.[1] Life expectancy, which was thirty to thirty-five years in 1800, increased to forty-five to fifty in 1900, and each year we are gaining three additional months. One girl out of every two born today will live to be a hundred. Longevity affects everyone, starting in childhood: it concerns not solely those who are reaching the end but people of all age groups. Knowing at the age of eighteen, as "millennials" do, that one might live for a century completely upends the conception of education, careers, the family and love affairs, making life a long, winding road that dawdles along, wanders, allows failures and repeated attempts. Now *we have time*: no point in hurrying to marry and procreate at twenty, to complete one's education too soon. We can pursue several educations, several occupations, several marriages. Society's ultimatums are less ignored than they are circumvented. We thereby acquire a virtue: indulgence toward our own hesitations. And a challenge: the terror of facing choices.

The swinging door

Fifty is the age when the brevity of life really begins. The human animal then experiences a kind of straddling. Formerly, time was movement toward an end; whether spiritual perfection or accomplishment, it was goal-directed. Now an unprecedented parenthesis has been opened between these two periods. What precisely is this parenthesis? A reprieve that leaves life open like a swinging door. An amazing advance that upsets everything, relations between generations, the status of salaried workers, marriage, the financing of social security, the cost of care for the old and infirm. A new category appears between maturity and old age: that of "seniors," to use the Latin term,[2] people in good physical condition and often better off than the rest of the population. It is the time when many people, having raised their children and performed their conjugal duties, get divorced or remarried. This change does not affect only the Western world: in Asia, Africa and Latin America, the decline in fertility is accompanied by the ageing of the population without the material conditions of this fact having been thought through.[3] Everywhere, public authorities are considering putting this fraction of the population back to work until the age of sixty-five or seventy. Old age is not the lot of only a small number of survivors; now, it is the future of a major part of humanity, with the sole exception of the American white working class, which is undergoing a worrisome increase in mortality.[4] By 2050, on a global scale, there are supposed to be twice as many old people as there are toddlers. In other words, there is no longer one but several old ages, and the only one that deserves that name is the one that immediately precedes death. We have to carry out a more refined division of the order of generations.

But brevity is also a factor of intensity and explains some people's feverish efforts to devour their remaining days, hastily trying to repair their failures or prolong what they have experienced. That is the advantage of countdowns: they make us eager to seize each passing moment. After the age of fifty, life is supposed to be requisitioned by urgency, possessed by an inexhaustible variety of appetites[5] – especially since we can be carried off at any time by an illness or an accident. From the fact that I exist now, "it does not follow that I must still exist afterward,"[6] wrote René Descartes. The uncertainty of tomorrow, despite medical progress, is no less tragic than it was in the seventeenth century and does not attenuate the precariousness of every new dawn. Longevity is a statistical truth, not a personal guarantee. We are making our way along a ridgeline that allows us to see the panorama on both sides.

Here we must distinguish between the future as a grammatical category and the future as an existential category; the latter implies a continued existence that is no longer contingent but wanted and desired. The former is undergone, the latter constructs; the former involves passivity, the latter conscious activity. Tomorrow it will be cold or rainy, but, whatever the weather, I will set out on the journey because I have decided to do so. One can remain alive very late, but does one still exist, in the sense in which Heidegger distinguished the being that consists in itself from the existent that projects itself forward?[7] For a man, "the heaviest burden is to live without existing," said Victor Hugo, more simply. What should we do with these extra twenty or thirty years that we have inadvertently acquired? There we are, like soldiers who are about to be demobilized and are enlisted for other battles. Basically, the chips are down, the time for settling accounts seems to have come, and yet we have to go on. Old age constitutes a paradoxical consolation for those who are afraid to live and who tell themselves that, over there, at the end of a long road, lies the Promised Land of Respite, where they can stop struggling and set down their burdens. Indian summer, that new, late autumn season, unprecedented in history, contradicts their hopes. They wanted to retire; they have to go on.

This reprieve, which is *a priori* empty of any content, is simultaneously exciting and alarming. The harvest of additional days has to be used. "My progress is to have discovered that I am no longer progressing," Sartre wrote in 1964, in his autobiography *Les Mots*.[8] He was then fifty-nine years old and confessed that he was nostalgic about "the young intoxication of the mountain climber." Is that where we still are, half a century later? The deadlines are getting shorter, the possibilities more limited, but there are still discoveries to be made, surprises and exhilarating love affairs to be had. Time has become a paradoxical ally: instead of killing us, it carries us; it is the vector of anguish and bliss, "half-orchard, half-desert" (René Char). Life lingers on, as do those long summer evenings when the fragrant air, exquisite food and convivial company make everyone want to prolong the magical moment and never retire to sleep.

Longevity is not a simple addition of years; it radically changes our relationship to life. First, it allows several diachronic humanities to cohabit on earth with different references and memories. What does a man who is almost a century old, who has known the period after World War I, World War II, the Cold War and the fall of the Berlin Wall, have in common with a child born in an environment of interconnected screens and hyper-technology? What do I have in common with myself, the man I used to be and the man I have become? Nothing more than an identity card. Chronologies collide with one another without being connected in any obvious way, and references diverge, creating real problems of translation between older and younger people: they no longer speak the same language. Longevity disarms incompatibles: today, it is possible to be one thing and another. A man can be a father, grandfather and great-grandfather, an old man and an athlete; a woman can be a mother and the bearer of her daughter's and her son-in-law's child. Methuselah is everywhere, but it's a petulant Methuselah: a man can procreate up to the age of seventy-five and engender a new child at the same time that his eldest gives him a grandchild, so that the uncle or aunt might then be forty years younger than their nephew or niece, and his youngest child half a century younger than his elder brother. Science allows veritable temporal permutations; lineages intertwine rather than succeeding one another, like the cables of a telephone switchboard; family hierarchies are overturned, and an abyss opens up in front of us and sweeps away all landmarks. If by chance centenarians were to become the majority, they would consider septuagenarians spoiled brats and cry: "Oh, these young people, they don't respect anything!"

This is the reprieve: *the provisional omission of the dénouement*, a fundamental uncertainty. Life is no longer an arrow that moves from birth to death but a "melodic duration" (Bergson), a multi-layered structure of superimposed temporalities. Rather than dream of time suspended ("Ô temps, suspends ton vol!," Lamartine asked. "How long?" Alain retorted), we now receive an unexpected gift. To enjoy a supplement is to cease mourning, like people with AIDS who have been saved at the last minute by antiretroviral therapy. The executioner has delayed the fall of his axe. The development of human life is exactly opposite to that of a whodunit: we know the end, we know who the killer is, but we have no desire to denounce him; on the contrary, we do everything we can to avoid unmasking him. As soon as he appears, we beg him: stay hidden; we still need many more years before finding you. The last chapter of a book can be as exciting as the earlier ones even if it recapitulates them.

If the privilege of youth is to remain undefined, it does not know what is going to happen, whereas that of Indian summer is to cheat with the conclusion. *It is the age of wavering between grace and collapse.* After fifty, insouciance is over, everyone has become more or less what he was supposed to become and now feels free to continue as he is or to reinvent himself.[9] Maturity aggregates in a single person dissimilar universes that post-maturity will mix up again, like a particle accelerator. An unprecedented adolescence, a belated puberty, as many people have emphasized: at the age of decline, it is no longer so much a matter of choosing one's life as it is of perpetuating it, changing its direction or enriching it. How to make good use of this remainder? "This is the first day of the rest of your life," the Anglo-Saxons say. The rest starts on the first day, but then it resembles opulence and later contracts. Time is like love in Plato, the child of poverty and abundance; it is the indispensable maturation, the fecund expectation that burgeons, but also erosion, exhaustion. To get old is to enter into the order of calculation: everything is limited, every passing day reduces our options, forces us to make choices.

But the fifty-year-old's paradoxical adolescence will not lead to any superior reason. Claude Roy speaks magnificently of "this way that life has of not finishing its sentences." It is human not to finish one's sentence, to leave it cracked open like a window. It is other people who will close it by inserting a period, not without arguing about our fate. In a famous book Kierkegaard distinguished three stages along the road of life: the aesthetic stage, that of immediacy; the ethical stage, that of moral requirement; and the religious stage, that of achievement.[10] The discussion is stimulating, but who could still divide his itinerary into three parts as distinct as the outline of a dissertation? Existence is a perpetual introduction to itself and remains so to the end; there is no gradation. We are at home in time only at the cost of being constantly expelled, thrown out of the present. We are long-term homeless people.

Cold shower

This fundamental deception remains: it is not life that science and technology have prolonged, it is old age. The real marvel would be to keep us at the gates of death in the condition and with the appearance of a thirty- or forty-year-old adult, hale and hearty, or to settle us forever in the age of our choice. Even if so-called life extension technology is working on this, through a series of treatments, surgeries and research on cells and mitochondria,[11] we are far from being able to achieve it. These sabbatical years are a poisoned gift: we live longer, but at the price of being ill, whereas life expectancy in good health has ceased rising.[12] Medicine has become a machine for fabricating handicaps and dementia.[13] We're being given twenty years of already worn-out life! We'd like to keep our preferred face, the one we chose among all those that evolution has accorded us, or get it back with a few strokes of the scalpel. Getting old is tolerable only if one remains decent in body and mind.

The fear of ageing thus increases as life gets longer and *ageing old age* gets further off. This fear appears earlier and earlier, begins in adolescence. Girls of twenty have their eggs frozen, begin plastic surgery, having their noses, lips, breasts and buttocks reshaped at the threshold of life. Surgery is becoming the obligatory accessory of a whole generation that dreams of metamorphoses at the risk of creating a humanity of clones. The anatomy received is not the anatomy dreamed of, and the anatomy dreamed of is never satisfied with the anatomy seen. Skin is never tight enough, re-densified or re-pulpified enough, the breasts never lifted enough, the cheekbones never prominent enough. The fear of not being in conformity is established at the end of infancy. The slightest sag requires a lift. So many ills have been conquered: we are astonished that they cannot all be immediately conquered. To the classical calamities is added that of not being able to overcome misfortune. The amazing advances in medicine make us imagine the virtual disappearance of adversity.

"Ageing will soon be a thing of the past," read a magazine headline in 1992.[14] Incredible news. If at that point the end of old age was already just a question of time, if we succeed in putting it off, turning back the biological clock, then the ultimate enemy, death, should soon be defeated. First we have to cure the mortal illness that is life, because the latter stops someday. We remain split between the fear of decrepitude and the mad hope of a miracle: the unreasonable certainty, thanks to the latest scientific developments, that we have overcome disease and death. We childishly dream of being spared, despite and against everything, and that the laws of longevity will finally be revealed – thanks, for example, to epigenetics or the DNA sequencing of supercentenarians.[15]

That is how we must understand the contemporary rebellion against death, of which transhumanism remains the main standard. Different kinds of modifiable inevitabilities are less and less often distinguished – slowing physical deterioration, prolonging life, inexorable inevitabilities, finitude and death. Death is no longer considered the normal end of a life but a therapeutic failure to be immediately corrected. The time will come when people are scandalized to learn they are dying, certain that the progress of research, within a few years, would have made it possible for them to live on. We are the victims of bad timing; the period owes it to us to cure us. Modernity has dangled before us the possibility of control over the living, of a "second creation" that would no longer owe anything to the vicissitudes of nature. It will no longer be these ambitions that seem crazy to us, but the delay or the obstacles to their realization. We have succeeded in "making the difference between the ideal and the real intolerable" (Marx), an attitude that can lead to reformative action or sterile recrimination.

By making longevity an absolute norm, civilization renders senility, the loss of capabilities and dependency more inadmissible. An unbearable observation: we continue to grow old and die. The fabulous promises made by the transhumanists, who want to remodel life with the help of biological engineering and artificial intelligence, have turned out, for the time being at least, to be agreeable speculations – *Faust* rewritten in digital language. They should be accused, not of being Promethean, but of not being Promethean enough. They have taken over communism's radiant future, but on scientific bases. It is the same consolation, the same dream of omniscience and omnipotence over oneself and over the world. For them, it is the body, "that anachronistic carapace," that has to be liquidated and remodeled in a new technological genesis.[16] We were flesh and viscera; let us become cyborgs and silicon. We are really clinging to the intersection of two mentalities: one classical, which assigns a destiny to each age, the other more recent, which rebels against this fatalism and wants to push back frontiers, improve the human being. This engineering seeking to remodel us, to augment us, arouses both our skepticism and our admiration. Transhumanism and biotechnologies elicit as much hatred as they do mad hopes. But, if they allow scientific research to move forward, why condemn them *a priori* and not show ourselves more pragmatic with regard to them?[17] We are promised that, before the middle of the century, research on senescent cells will allow us to reach the age of 150. Why not? We will no longer be there to see it, but good luck to our descendants.

We were promised eternity next year; grief-struck minds actually mourned the death of death, and we registered the gap between the ambitions declared and the results recorded. The inevitable has not been abolished, it has been put off: in Germany and Japan, more diapers are sold for the elderly than for babies! Let us not add to the distress of getting old the absurdity of denying its sadness or promising its abolition. Our power, which is both considerable and risible, is to delay its effects, to slow the damage: this margin is the space of our freedom. Without taking into account that, at this time of life, the black hole of depression often stalks the firmest characters. An improvement of the status of the elderly can be expected not only from progress in research but also from progress in mentalities.

However that may be, the body does not lie; the body commands. It tells us: the future is still possible, but on my conditions. If you don't respect me, you'll pay dearly for it. Starting at the age of forty-five, medicine explains to us, the human being lives with a gun to his head. It is up to him to delay the shot or pull the trigger. Here we must distinguish between the inherited body and the experienced body, which is above all a vulnerable body, constantly patched up, like an old, elegant sedan that breaks down and that we obstinately repair until the next accident. There comes a time when health consists in moving from one illness to another, without illusions, when healing is slower and convalescence longer, which avoids the dangerous predominance of a single pathology and divides up the threat among several of them.

YOU SAY IT TO YOURSELF

Know your place: that's what has been drummed into us since we were children. Don't show off, don't put on airs. Ne pète plus haut que ton cul ("Don't fart higher than your ass"), to use that delightful French expression that dates from 1640. Each of us is supposed to have a place assigned to us by his parents, his original milieu, his education. Trying to reach another level of success, of wealth, would be to forget where one came from and who one is. Woe to him who transgresses that rule! The humble, the disinherited should not try to parade about above their means, to become slaves to social illusions. This warning becomes more serious with age. One is born a woman or a Jew or a black, but we all get old someday (Pascal Champvert). And this development immediately puts us in a reserved pigeonhole: that of adults who have done their time and have to give way in their turn.

In general, to live is never to know one's place and stay there. Our center of gravity is located outside us, in situations that fatalism deems inaccessible. Each soul contains in itself powers whose extent it does not suspect. Whoever aspires to a tranquil life can lead it as he wishes, especially after the age of sixty, choosing a sedentary existence, a chastened imagination, and the bitter pleasure of anticipated fiascos. Certain people allow themselves to wither in the middle of life. Humanity is divided into two families, the hermetically sealed and the exposed. Over time, the number of the former increases vertiginously. For the latter, the ambition to open themselves out again, to travel the globe in every direction, may lead them to disillusionment, but also to a searing intensity and enthusiasm.

"He's speaking out of turn" – that's how we censure those who seek to rise beyond their condition. We say it to ourselves at every age: without these subterfuges that raise us to another altitude, that lead us into the fabulous lands of our imagination, we could simply not tolerate the tedious babble of our lives. We envelop our slightest acts and projects in a narrative and poetic fabric that magnifies them. Restlessness and romanticism: these maladies of adolescence are those that accompany us throughout life. Right to the end, we dream of our existences having the consistency of a fiction. "The conquest of the superfluous provides a spiritual excitement greater than that of the conquest of the necessary. Man is a creation of desire, not a creation of need."[18]

Wisdom or resignation?

When time shortens, we have to create a provisional morality. A person in his fifties today is in the same situation as a newborn in the Renaissance: his life expectancy, in good health, is about thirty years, the equivalent of a whole life for a European three centuries ago. He becomes, in spite of himself, a prophet of the short term. Finding oneself confined in this way increases the desire to live. Age has gradually ceased to be a verdict; it is no longer the threshold beyond which the human being is considered to be out of service because, until his last moments, he can still modify his destiny. "To grow old is gradually to withdraw from appearance," said Goethe. It is excellent that nowadays people over fifty do not wish to sit on the bench, but to continue to appear, to actively oppose the discriminations of which they are the object, even when they represent nearly 30 percent of the population. They fight relentlessly to remain in the light and to avoid sinking into the category of the Invisibles.

To get old is in principle to enter the period of answers finally acquired and found. We are supposed to know and understand. But the answers fail to exhaust the wealth of the questions. A good life is a well-posed question that indefinitely postpones its clarification. In societies that used to be oral, such as those of West Africa, every elder, having received initiation and being able to talk with the dead, was supposed to incarnate a treasure of spirituality. "When an old man dies, it is a library that is burned," wrote the Malian writer Hampâté Bâ in 1960. Too often, in our cultures, it's a scratched record that stops. Old age is traditionally opposed to rapidity: it walks at a senatorial pace; it has taken the time to reflect and ponder its decisions. But, at that time in life as well, the predominant feeling is that time is moving very fast, that days are collapsing one on another like a house of cards, and that from now on we will have to count in quarters, in months, even in weeks. Great age seems to be a paradox: *an acceleration that is slowing down.*

The autumn of life has always been defined in contradictory ways: the sweet pleasure of dying surrounded by the esteem and respect of all, but also by the sadness of a life that stays close to the ground, an endless hibernation in decline. On this subject, we oscillate between prudent praise and denigration, admiration and repulsion. Especially since the senior citizen now owes his longevity only to the progress of medicine[19] and not to his merits alone. Senior citizens used to be rare, haloed with a certain prestige; now they are legion. But they are floating seniors, incapable of defining their status or delimiting the fateful cycles. "Don't miss life's radiant month of June,"[20] said Vladimir Jankélévitch. But the months of September, October and December can also be magnificent, even if they seem less sunny.

Classically, old age was the time when things calmed down – the time when grandparents welcomed their grandchildren with the loving kindness of those who can understand everything and pardon anything. In it, the essential was separated from the accessory: the desiccation of the body left only what mattered most, spiritual grandeur and the beauty of the soul. Life grew narrower; it consisted entirely in a flame, but that flame was sublime, inspiring the respect and admiration of all. This model has been blurred: the life that remains active is contrasted with the wheezy life that we push away like a ghost, that of the bedridden old man in the grip of extinction. He puts all his energy into self-preservation; holding on is a daily battle won over the dislocation of the body by illness.[21]

Another cliché is superimposed on this one: great age is supposed to be the time to free oneself, stage by stage, from an excessive appetite for earthly pleasures, to devote oneself to meditation, to study, to delivering oracles in the form of definitive maxims, the better to prepare oneself for the Big Departure. It is not certain that any of our contemporaries find such a farewell attractive. In fact, the secret of a happy old age resides in doing precisely the opposite: *cultivating until late in life all our passions, all our abilities, not giving up any pleasure, any curiosity, setting impossible challenges for ourselves, continuing, right to the end, to love, work, travel, and remain open to the world and to other people.* In a word, testing our unimpaired powers.

What do we have to give up if we want to keep what is essential? First of all, the imperative of renunciation that associates age with the gradual diminution of our desires. Even if it ends up defeating us and depriving us of ourselves, old age must be reconstructed. The dictate that orders us to stay in bed, to resign ourselves, has to be challenged: classical wisdom may be simply another name for resignation. We have to resist with all our strength the impoverishment of existence, relegation in rest homes with flowery names that are in fact medicalized death houses. In earlier times, people came into existence without a model: the novels of education or apprenticeship that emerged in the eighteenth century helped individuals find their way in the labyrinth of the years, to move from the particular to the universal as the dislocation of the *Ancien Régime* increased. Now we enter the autumn of life without a guide, because this period did not exist as such until the middle of the twentieth century. So we should speak of novels of de-education that disaccustom us to the ways we have learned, detox us from immemorial twaddle. We may have to become calmer as we grow old, but not resigned. Thus we are torn between two kinds of wisdom: saddened acceptance of the inevitable and joyful approval of possibilities. We balance one against the other. Since Freud, we know that, in the unconscious, time does not pass;[22] it is we who pass into it, it is the registry office that assigns us a date of birth. Age is a social convention backed by a biological reality. It is always possible to reorient the convention. In the end, of course, we will be defeated. The essential thing is *to refuse to interiorize our defeat and to keep on doing so right to the end.*

CHAPTER 2

Staying in the Dynamics of Desire

I find my last years fascinating. I don't feel old at all, except
when I'm shaving and look at myself in the mirror.

KEITH RICHARDS

Beyond a certain age, we can all be overcome by a
feeling of usurpation, as if we were stealing the bread of
the following generations. Not only have our ancestors,
through their efforts, bequeathed us an excessive degree
of comfort, but we also seem to enjoy this advantage at
the expense of our children and grandchildren. According
to an indestructible proverb attributed sometimes to the
Indian chief Seattle, sometimes to Saint-Exupéry: "We do
not inherit the earth from our parents, we borrow it from
our children." Thus we would be the cannibal generation
that takes advantage of both sides of history, leaving
behind us an immense debt and granting ourselves privileges that are just so many larcenies. And our successors
have the feeling that they live less well than we do. In
addition, they curse us for our role in what awaits them

– the destruction of their health, of their illusions. Isn't it time for us to make our exit?

Retreat or disaster?

To counter this resentment, there is only one solution: putting sexagenarians and older people back to work – on a voluntary basis.[1] The constitution of a whole age group as a leisure class, focused solely on consumerism, is a catastrophe that was carried out in our societies, with all the best intentions, after World War II. Experience and perspicacity usually increase over the years: staying in or returning to an activity means putting people in connection with others, in service to others, making them actors in the full sense of the term. It means doing away with the prejudice that regards elders as a class of parasites whose eclipse is eagerly awaited to make room for their juniors. Paul Lafargue, a revolutionary communist, Karl Marx's son-in-law and the author of *The Right to be Lazy*, is supposed to have invented consumer society: in his ideal city, an iron law forbids working for more than three hours; machines will produce by themselves all the necessary opulence, and the rest of the time men and women will feast, put on shows to make fun of the earlier world, and enjoy an endless vacation.[2] By a strange twist of history, this buffoonish utopia, which praises a permanent void in distraction, was to triumph first in the very capitalist North America, which in the twentieth century invented the empire of entertainment, though it did not do away with the role of labor.

From the outset, there was an ambiguity about retirement. It is said that the German chancellor Bismarck, who invented the old-age pension program in 1889 and was eager to cut the ground from under the social democrats' feet, asked a statistician: "At what age can we set retirement so that we don't have anything to pay?" The expert is supposed to have replied: "At sixty-five, your honor." Most government employees died before reaching that age.[3] We are willing to provide workers with pensions if they die early. But if they have the temerity to live on for two or three decades, the machine jams and becomes a financial black hole. This social welfare achievement, made in France in 1945, also produced the ageing that it is supposed to relieve.[4] Some demanding tasks require an early retirement for a body worn out by repetitive work. But, for others, this retirement is a *twofold penalty*, the conjunction of impoverishment and old age, the exit from active working life accompanied by a decreased income, the "marriage of hunger and thirst," as an old proverb has it. Obligatory retirement at the age of sixty, modulated differently depending on the occupation, plunges us into the curse of absolute leisure erected into a way of life as if whole groups of elderly people were to be thrust back into the infantile universe of the amusement park. This free time is usually spent not broadening one's horizons but, rather, sitting hypnotized in front of screens: growing old means binge-watching and surfing the internet. The nightmare of "gated communities" in the United States, those old people's gulags that are cut off from the rest of the world and forbidden to children and young adults. The idea that work is a pie of a fixed size that has to be divided up among everyone is part of a Malthusian economics; on the contrary, work is a flexible quantity that can always be changed, depending on a country's innovation and dynamism. The young and the old do not have the same competencies, and the latter can complement each other rather than cancel each other out. It is stupidly postulated, especially in France, that no authentic destiny has any connection with work, and that one has to wait until a certain age before beginning to enjoy life. It is heartbreaking to see people in their thirties and forties dreaming of retiring at sixty in order finally to be able to enjoy their free time: real life is here, now, right away, despite the drudgery, constraints and obstacles. Leisure then becomes an activity that they stubbornly work at, the better to mourn their earlier careers. Adults who are perfectly healthy in body and mind are tossed in the trash, where after a few months of inertia they waste away or sink into depression. Not to mention this new example: that of the house husband who is over sixty-five, an unproductive drone whose wife, younger than he, continues to work and bring home a pay check. The success of the "Yellow Vests" in France in the autumn of 2018 is explained in part by the active role played by these protesters in their sixties and seventies who gathered at roundabouts, finally wrenched away from their solitude and vacuity. These gray-haired anarchists rediscovered for a few months a sense of life, of being useful. During this May 1968 for retired people, they emerged *from the nightmare of obligatory idleness.*

Polls assure us that we feel happiest at around seventy,[5] thanks to detachment and good humor when coping with stress. Maybe – but isn't this detachment connected with the fact that we have left the world, that we have been deprived of any lever for acting on it? Are we really more blooming at seventy than at forty because we have been freed from material things?[6] A correlation between stopping work and tranquillity of mind is postulated, forgetting the demonstrations of retired people protesting against the erosion of their pensions and the feeling of emptiness that follows the cessation of activity. Then the conjunction of poverty and old age is painted in the colors of jubilation.

In the 1970s Simone de Beauvoir described a fifty-year-old woman who had lost her economic independence and was the victim of an empty availability: she no longer had any obligations, her children were grown up, the grand-mother's role had few attractions for her. She remained in full possession of her financial means but was vegetating in a desert of boredom. "She contemplated the long years without prospects that remained to her and murmured: 'No one needs me.'" She felt useless. That word applies to all those who once had a job. The experience acquired, the competencies demonstrated are disqualified on the grounds that room has to be made for younger people who are eager to prove themselves – a genuine devastation for those who are forced to stop when they were not asking for either calm or peace and wanted to remain active in their domain. *The truth of a fulfilled life lies in the test that fortifies and not in the repose that weakens.* The retiree is past his prime in the eyes of society but still hale and hearty in his own. Freedom, which in adults is masked by various occupational and familial responsibilities, returns to him, as attractive as it is terrifying. Then he has to find new reasons to live, besides simple entertainment or charity work. It is one thing to establish a "time bank," as Sweden has to allow employees to take a break of a few sabbatical years[7] or a breather during a career; it is another to force retirement on people who do not wish to retire on the grounds that they have passed their expiry date.[8] A temporary suspension is not the equivalent of forced relaxation. Retreat: a perfect example of a great victory that has been transformed into a calamity for its beneficiaries.

The philosophical age

To advance in life is to recite a list of disasters so obvious that it would be tedious to enumerate them. But, by thus attaching oneself to the catalogue of penances, one misses the essential point: we are living better and better and to older and older ages. At the age when our ancestors were already entering the shadows, there is a joy mixed with anxiety in feeling oneself exist, in having escaped the most serious illnesses. It is the absurd joy of being still alive, of inhabiting one's body, even if it is somewhat worn out. Not everything is still possible, but much remains permissible. In 1922, the Goncourt prize was awarded not to Roland Dorgelès, the war veterans' spokesman, but to Marcel Proust. The next day, the headline in the communist newspaper *L'Humanité* read: "Make way for the old guys!" Proust was only forty-eight. Today, who would describe a man or woman of forty-eight as "old"? It's after fifty that we really have our lives in front of us, when we can finally enjoy the youth we missed out on at twenty because we had to earn diplomas, look for a job, prove ourselves, excuse ourselves for being greenhorns, emerge from childhood, get through the tormented first love affairs, and carry all alone the burden of a brand new freedom. Finding oneself, making mistakes, choosing among options, none of which pleases us, being told every morning that we don't realize how lucky we are – what a nightmare all that is, when you think about it! Then we construct ourselves by destroying ourselves with alcohol, drugs, excesses of all kinds in the name of conformism, social pressure. Youth has beauty, energy and curiosity, but it is an imitative age that gropes its way forward, stumbles, succumbs to fads, to ideologies. Maturity is practical, but it has lost youth's alacrity and energy. As we grow up, we never cease to encounter advantages and disadvantages, always out of tune, always awkward.

In our latitudes, life happens only once: there are no classes to make up for lost time like those in Buddhism and Hinduism. With the notion of *karma*, these two religions invented destiny on a trial basis: in our current state we pay for our earlier errors and purify ourselves, cycle after cycle, of our weaknesses until we are freed of them. The East seeks to free itself *from* this life; the West seeks to free itself *in* this life. For the East, the only remedy is not to be reborn; for the West, it is to be resuscitated several times in the course of a single period of time. The Christian stakes his eternity on the short term, whereas the Hindu, to escape the pain of being, has at his disposal a quantity of successive incarnations in the course of which his soul is purified. As soon as Europe tore itself away from the grip of the Middle Ages, at the transition from the fourteenth to the fifteenth century, and from a predestined world in which everyone is a prisoner of his status, his religion and his origins, a new promise emerged: humans were henceforth seen as the creators of their own destiny and their own time. They are supposed to be capable of challenging social, psychological and biological boundaries and to have entered the era of indefinite self-construction. The myth of the "self-made man" in the United States is based on these promises. But the latter are far from having been kept, and the curse of determinisms remains all the stronger because we think we have eliminated them. It remains that the modernity that arose from the Enlightenment is still admirable because it is a collective revolt against fate.

The third age is the philosophical age, the age of the Mind par excellence, now more than ever. In it, all the challenges of the human condition are posed in their most acute form, as they were defined by Kant: what am I allowed to hope for, what am I allowed to know, to believe? The Indian summer is truly a "conversation that the soul carries on with itself" (Socrates, *Theatetus*), a state of permanent self-examination. In it the active life can alternate with the contemplative life. It constitutes the

31

moment when we confront the tragic structure of existence without a mask or blinders, a boundary situation. "By the time you've learned how to live, it's already too late,"[9] said Aragon. But life is not an academic subject, because it never ceases to change the conditions for learning it. If the display of talents is for youth and consists in realizing all a person's potential, old age can also be seen as the last age of education rather than as a dead end. The power of dissolution of the passing years does not exclude a certain dynamism, even if it is restrained. We persist in growing with an eye to the future, even if time is shrinking. At all times, we are the sole artisans of our salvation, including in the choice of our death.

We always remain alumni of the school of life, and this will to learn is a sign precisely of freshness of mind. The initiation will continue even unto the tomb. We can combine the pleasure of teaching with that of being taught, of taking courses and giving them, of being the one who professes and the one who asks questions, in perfect reciprocity. We still have enough time to open ourselves again to the world, to start learning again. We have been made, perhaps, but we are still imperfect. Real life is not absent, because there is no "real" life, only many interesting avenues that remain to be explored.

What shall we do with our twenty years (of additional life)?

We resent our elders for showing us the path we don't want to take. They prefigure what we are going to become – machines, cyborgs – because beyond the age of fifty we all enter more or less into the age of prostheses, glasses, hearing aids, valves, implants, various kinds of chips, etc.

In an individualistic society we are offered at least two models, which can be combined as we wish: playing the old scamp or striking the pose of the disillusioned sage, the provider of oracles, wavering between infantilism and solemnity. Setting no limits to one's appetites, returning at the age of sixty to teenage dreams, or deciding that the chips are down and withdrawing into the group of little old men who play cards or shuffleboard while waiting for supper. On the one hand is the tribe of retirees who constantly pop vitamins and are often in better shape than younger people, having succeeded in overcoming various maladies. Rather well off, if they belong to the middle or upper classes, they want to sink their teeth into life and show a fierce energy at an age when their ancestors were already senile or bedridden. On the other hand, there is the gray clan of the resigned, who want to avoid the tumult. Follies of the heart and mind may strike at any time, for both sexes. The appearance of Viagra and, for women, hormonal treatments offers august sexagenarians intoxicating powers that disturb the peace of the lower regions. How many old married couples split up when one of them, breaking the truce of chastity, rediscovers a taste for amorous jousting. The generation of 1968 has experienced two miracle pills, contraceptives and vasodilators. The gluttony of elderly people eager to roll the dice one last time, to throw themselves into sports, travel, work or saturnalia of the flesh, comes from the new temporal strategic depth that is offered to each of us: in Europe, the average age of maternity has reached thirty years, and the onset of menopause may someday be pushed beyond sixty. A pathetic prospect? Maybe. But to reproach the elderly for their inappropriate lusts, their desire to undertake projects, to continue to work, is to condemn them to a premature death, and to condemn oneself as soon as one has reached that borderline. What is finer than to short-circuit temporal sequences, to thumb one's nose at destiny, to accord oneself, at least for a short time, an excess of intoxication, sensations, encounters? Life is an uncertainty that lasts and that, as long as it lasts, guarantees that we are alive.

We constantly oscillate between *the promise and the program, between energy and entropy*: to be born is to be promoted to the promise of a future that we don't know, whereas we are predestined to disappear like an image that fades as it is reproduced over and over, because our cells repeat themselves imperfectly as they renew themselves. So long as the promise wins out over the program, we can keep going. We have certainly not asked to be born; but, as we advance in age, we transform this arbitrary gift into a right, and we demand to persevere in being as long as possible. "You have to be a real drunkard to drink the dregs when you've finished the bottle ... Living is not excruciating but it is superfluous,"[10] wrote Seneca in an aphorism that foreshadows Cioran. But, apart from the fact that the weariness of being may strike us even in childhood, there is something magnificent about staying on for one last lap.

Now whole generations of pseudo-adults are coming along, wrinkled schoolchildren who toy with fate and with years. They seem to have moved directly from puberty to senility, omitting maturity. They remain young until they become old. The Great Recommencement and the Great Rejuvenation, and not the Eternal Return, constitute the only form of eternity we found when the belief in Paradise faded among the faithful. The classical Christian trinity, Hell, Purgatory and Paradise, came back down to earth and now shares our secular lives: the beyond is here on earth, shared out and cut up into periods. The existence of a man or woman contains several lives, and they pile up without resembling one another. They form a continuous creation that is sedimented and superimposed in the form of a destiny. We make mistakes, correct them, make others, in a series of failures that end up composing a fine career. And, since there is no longer any model of a good life after sixty, it's up to each person to create it. We are more than ever like Peter Pan, children who don't want to grow up, senior citizens who don't want to grow old.[11] We sow our wild oats out of sync with the biological clock: young people shack up at the age of twenty, whereas their graying parents lark about and multiply affairs. Reason does not grow along with the number of years; middle-aged lust can strike even on the threshold of death. The noisy exuberance of old age may seem ridiculous, or even exasperating, but do we prefer that the elderly gradually slip toward the grave or the aseptic hospital? What is more exhilarating than breaking the rules?

That is what's at stake: will this new age be a transfigured maturity or a post-adolescence quavering at the edge of the abyss? It will very probably be a tension between these two states, an accepted schizophrenia. On the one hand – and this is the benefit of old age – a growing taste for nature, study, silence, meditation, contemplation; on the other hand, a still strong and even renewed attachment to pleasure in all its forms. Improvising a new life at fifty-five or sixty is not the same thing as setting out on life at sixteen. Will the new seniors be the guardians of trans-mission or "old satyrs used up by debauchery" (Rousseau), 73-year-old, narcissistic scoundrels like Donald Trump or august ancestors with white beards? The spark of passions remains alive, the soul and heart are still prompt to catch fire: the spiritual and sentimental age does not coincide with the biological age. There is only one way to slow ageing, and that is to remain in the dynamics of desire. A reconciliation of incompatibles: romanticism and carpet slippers, debauchery and wrinkles, gray hair and desired storms of emotion. We have not found the solution to the misfortunes of the human condition, only opened a tiny window in the cave. "People aren't serious when they're seventeen," sang Rimbaud. We aren't serious at fifty, either, or at sixty or seventy, even if decorum urges us to look as if we were. Age has to be stripped of its decrepit ornaments; ageing has to be turned against itself, with humour and elegance. Limits exist to be pushed. At every stage of its development, life fights back against the irreversible – and goes on fighting until it plunges into the abyss.

YOU HAVEN'T CHANGED AT ALL!

To tell someone, "You haven't changed at all," is discreetly to request reassurance. Whether we are in our thirties or our sixties, we are asking our inter-locutor to return the compliment, to certify that we are really in the same time zone. To meet an old friend whom one hasn't seen for years is to undertake an operation of facial recognition, like witnesses who have to identify, behind a one-way mirror, the perpetrator of an assault. Memory begins a rapid calculation, picking out in the face that is presented the features that might awaken recollection: it subtracts the current face from the old one, summons up two different periods and compares them. The person protests – "Hey, it's me!" – and the eyes sound the alarm, begging you to make the connection. The face is what we share with all our peers. That is why we couldn't see it forgotten without irreparable damage.

"You don't look your age" means: you haven't bowed your head to nature's dictates; you've played a trick on convention. There is stupor and almost anger on encountering, on a street corner, a person of our own generation who seems to be our father or grandfather: it's not possible that this ruin is my contemporary! Time, that great demolisher, usually takes pleasure in deforming features, crushing them or distending them, without indulgence. It places a magnifying glass on faces, making one feature bigger, reconfiguring a physiognomy, wrinkling the skin, covering it with spots, thinning the hair, enlarging the cheekbones, lengthening the nose or the ears, undertaking a monstrous morphing. The human face is a palimpsest on which several periods are superimposed: in an old friend of whom we used to be fond, we rediscover the adolescent's wild laugh and the scattered remains of an abundant head of hair. We are surrounded by people scrutinizing us, analyzing us with an imperious air. They want to extract confessions from our appearance.

"You've remained just the same" thus means: you are the witness to our old world; you are the proof that we shared the energy for which I'm still nostalgic. Old age cloaks us in a deceptive resemblance to ourselves. We no longer distinguish the person who looks out at us from the mirror every morning: who are you, and what do you want from me? Age seems to have taken hold of us by surprise; another self has been born from us who isn't us. That's what destiny is, said Hegel: oneself in the form of another. We think of advertising films that show, in accelerated form, a whole human life, from the cradle to the grave. Childish smiles at hunched old couples walking hand in hand on a beach. A fairy world and a *danse macabre* combined. In this

37

case, it is the compression of an existence into a few minutes that is frightening: we have hardly had time to taste life, to savor its bitterness and its delights, before we have become an old gentleman or an old lady very different from what we used to be.

PART II

Life Always Begun Again

CHAPTER 3

The Saving Routine

You don't admire as you should the
stunning miracle that life is.

ANDRÉ GIDE, *LES NOURRITURES TERRESTRES*

Describing his passion as an inveterate smoker, Zeno, an amiable pensioner in Trieste in the Austro-Hungarian Empire at the end of the nineteenth century who is tired of coughing up his lungs, is possessed by a desire for health. He divides his time between visits to doctors and psychoanalysts and stays in nursing homes, where electric shocks are used to wean him off smoking. But he inevitably relapses. "I believe the taste of a cigarette has a more intense flavor when it's your last."[1] He's been smoking his last cigarette for fifty-four years, and, as melancholic as he is amused, he has to admit that, "With me, things are often repeated."[2]

"It is enough to be" (Madame de Lafayette)

Repetition does not have good press among Moderns. It is doubly disqualified since Romanticism and the invention of psychoanalysis. Classicism was based on the certainty of an ideal past: the Ancients had attained perfection in all domains, and it sufficed to imitate them. Innovation was considered inappropriate, and the notion of plagiarism was meaningless, since intellectual property did not exist: on the contrary, one had to draw on the treasury of tales, stories and fables available to all and not hesitate to reproduce them, to use them to make collages and montages. La Fontaine endlessly rewrote Aesop, an emancipated slave of the seventh century BCE, and Johann Sebastian Bach drew shamelessly on Vivaldi's concertos for violins, to copy and retranscribe them as concertos for the harpsichord. A good text and a good piece of music resounded from all the earlier writings and scores and sometimes added a little more – the grace of a variation, of a commentary. Pillaging and counterfeiting, far from being punished, were recommended. Artists reinvented on the basis of a preceding pastiche. In Antiquity, some went so far as to attribute to an Ancient a book that they themselves had written, to spread a new message by the procedure known as pseudepigraphy.[3] (That is the procedure that Jean Potocki chose in the *Manuscript trouvé à Saragosse* in 1810, and many authors, fearing the censors, resorted to the same stratagem.) A good Christian was supposed to live in accord with *The Imitation of Christ*, an anonymous work of piety written and rewritten starting in the fifteenth century, to win his salvation and purify his soul.

Inversely, Romanticism, a wayward child of 1789, celebrated originality, the result of individual creation. Poets, musicians, painters and playwrights were to upset the codes, pulverize ossified traditions, create amid noisy quarrels and transgression. And just as artists plumbed "the depths of the unknown to find something new" (Baudelaire), it was necessary to flee bourgeois mediocrity, which was enslaved to calculation and commerce. Rejected by the nobility and the proletariat for its cupidity, the bourgeoisie was, in the eyes of the bohemians, marked by ontological baseness. Since its morality had reduced desire to the dimensions of material enrichment alone, its life was methodical, guided by the appetite for profit and a taste for acquisition. From that point on, the rebel or creator had to distinguish himself from this pettiness and, rather than withering on the vine, set out in search of turbulence, fury and grandeur.

Two things date from Romanticism and its hatred for conformity: the dream of immortality was replaced by that of *posterity*, a belated recognition of *artistes maudits* who were ahead of their time, which has now been eclipsed by *notoriety*, namely self-inflation on all the networks and media as a visible, floating ego. Finally, it was in the nineteenth century that the praise of those on the margins (migrants, sexual and racial minorities, prisoners, criminals) began and had the effect of destroying the norm, a development that a trend exploited by late twentieth-century philosophers such as Derrida, Deleuze, Guattari and Foucault. The bourgeois, as we know, have changed, because they in turn have become bohemians, wanting to be "workers by day and party animals by night" (Daniel Bell). Whether on the left or the right, they hope to enjoy their social status and at the same time take advantage of the emancipation of mores, at the risk of living in a cultural contradiction. That is why the philosophy of intensity is now conveyed by the big multinationals on the basis of Nietzschean mottoes ("Become what you are," "Whatever doesn't kill you makes you stronger"). By a strange reversal, Nietzsche has become the main provider of these companies' advertising slogans. The adulator of the superman is above all the philosophical guarantor of the consumerist superman who creates himself on the basis of what he buys, wears or eats.

As for Freud, he discerns in repetition a compulsion that leads the patient endlessly to repeat the same scenarios of romantic or professional failures. The symptom serves to screen a deeper anxiety that prevents healing and preserves the trauma as much as it manifests it. Some absurd manias that isolate us from others may deprive us of great pleasures, but they protect us against greater anxieties. They become defensive rituals that shelter us from the event, whatever it might be. Better to waste away from exhaustion than to open up to the unknown.

And yet we have to sing the praises of habit. It is the attire we give our acts, the habitat that structures us, the mental fabric of our lives. It constitutes the internal disposition that has become second nature and spares us many psychic expenses. We are never anything but the creatures of our habits, which are more difficult to uproot than a belief. Regularity is death, the avant-gardes claim; that is to forget that it constitutes the ontological basis of our destinies and the condition of our survival. To try to abolish it, to fly the double banner of unpredictability and perpetual invention, may be to disrupt life's dreadful banality, but it is above all to make it impossible. "To live without dead time and enjoy without limits," to adopt the situationists' old commercial slogan, is to run the risk of transforming intensity into routine, into an agreed convulsion. When life is frozen solid like an iced-up brook or a botoxed face, it is tempting to dream of a total change – of partner, of occupation, of country. But this fantasy of an absolute transmutation is above all an excellent way of putting up with one's condition. It elicits a reinforcement of the status quo: the more we complain, the more we endure, and we complain only in order to change nothing.

From childhood on, we fabricate traditions. What we call routine is not an unfortunate accident befalling beings without a history; it is the armature without which we couldn't hold up, the set of automatic reflexes that construct us and constrain us at the same time. Life depends on invisible threads that enclose us and support us without our knowing it and end up breaking, one by one. Not everything that is immobile is at rest, Aristotle said. For an event to rise up in the dullness of daily routine, empty hours – neutral duration – are necessary to move time along, without grandeur. Staggering moments almost always occur against a background of minor concerns from which they stand out. Without monotony, no overwhelming events are possible. Our everyday life is a *basso continuo* from which a few stunning arias occasionally emerge.

The splendor of the trivial

A fundamental question after the age of fifty: what keeps us going, gets us out of bed every morning, happy to return to the world? When they're twenty, people want to force open the future, cause something extraordinary and extravagant to happen. Then, they see routine life as an abomination that they'd like to subject to a continual effervescence. In its most radical form, this utopia was realized by totalitarian states that plunged their citizens into terror and war. The will to destroy the status quo, the refusal to compromise "with ludicrous conditions, in this world, all through life" (André Breton), may lead teenagers to have a powerful desire to breach the dikes. How can we fail to understand that impulse? With rare exceptions, our lives are not novels because they remain desperately unchanging. Everyday life is an attenuation of anecdotes; nothing, or nearly nothing, happens. Our lives become poor in events. The question "What's new?" always elicits the same response: "Nothing special." But we exist only if we can talk about ourselves, deal out our everyday lives in the form of anecdotes, no matter how derisory they may be. The challenge of banality is to keep on course through the mild storm of hours that follow one another, all the same, with their power to discompose and discourage the most steadfast hearts.

In this regard, the genre of autofiction, an annex to autobiography, created in 1977 by Serge Doubrovsky, is in fact an attempt to extract a narrative from the platitude of our lives. We don't relate what we have experienced, we write in order to understand ourselves better, to persuade ourselves that we are alive. We represent ourselves to amplify ourselves, even minimally; we are dazzled by the inexhaustible wealth harbored by an apparently ordinary destiny. And the private diary also invents its own reader, a fellow in banality, who takes joy in seeing the author rack up, week after week, such ridiculous and precious harvests. It creates a community of destiny between the writer and the reader, who get drunk on sharing such an absence of adventures. This penury seems to them an unrecognized plethora: the most insignificant minute, the slightest pleasures are still rich with an inexhaustible variety of occurrences. Countless possible presences throb in a day's long stretches of emptiness; they must be re-exhumed like a diamond imprisoned in its gangue. The thinner the destiny, the thicker the fiction when it enters into the infinitely small, teases out minuscule nuances, raises the negligible to the rank of a tragedy. To magnify is to rediscover the splendor of the ordinary, which is nothing more than an unexplored giddiness. Even on low-energy days, miniature hurricanes are generated. The completely insignificant is also provided with a narrative structure. That's the essence of the novel: the fiction of a desire loaded with that blissful burden, the narrative.

Starting at a certain age, continuity takes priority over admirable novelty: the concern is no longer so much to change life as to preserve what is best in it. Youth asks: must we fulfill ourselves or transcend ourselves? First of all, maturity replies, we have to maintain ourselves. Montaigne cites Augustus's minister Maecenas:

> Make me lame in hand,
> Lame in foot and thigh,
> Shake out my loosened teeth:
> While life stays, so stay I.

He concludes: "So bewitched are men by their wretched existence, that there is no condition so harsh that they will not accept it to keep alive."[4] In a whole life that lasts, the past seems an inverted prophecy that foreshadows the present, and the present seems a retrospective that has been confirmed. We have been right to behave as we have. The sempiternal murmur of existence is no longer a proof of weakness but one of self-confidence.

Our view of the past is divided between two clichés: it was either a series of wonders, after which interest declines ("it was better before," as people say), or the imperfect preface to a future that will fulfill it. The first conception is that of the conservative, the second that of the progressive. Reduced to the personal level, such a version sinks into nostalgia – the past was magnificent – or leads to an escape toward an idealized future. With age, this problem can be inverted: everything has already been done, and yet everything remains to be done or redone. Our great pleasure is then recognizing as much as it is exploring: as in children's stories, we enjoy rediscovering things even more than being surprised, or, rather, the surprise has to be enveloped in the veils of a certain familiarity. We want to feel the same expectations, the same thrills, even though we know what is going to happen. *It is the comfort of reassuring repetition.* Hearing beloved voices again, our favorite musical or film genres, familiar melodies, the usual faces, the sonorities of our language. Just as there is a chemical formula for every perfume, we find, starting in middle age, the formula that suits us, and we no longer want to change it. Even if we remain tempted by the prospect of the great upheaval, we know better than before *what it is important to safeguard, what it is permissible to hope for, and unreasonable to desire.*

Here begins the new life

Each day is like a total human drama: it constitutes a symbolic division of existence, with its radiant dawn, its triumphant noon, its busy afternoon, its serene twilight. The sleeper's awakening in the morning is a small daily resurrection of the dead: it brings us to light, restores to us the strengths that night had taken away from us. Nature continues to set the rhythm of our lives, whether we want it to or not, just as our moods are influenced by the grayness or the splendor of the sky. Therein lies the connection between the microcosm that we are and the overall macrocosm. The weather causes our bodies to swim in a great meteorological envelope that partly determines our sorrows or our joys. Light fills us with bliss, while a dark sky weighs on us like a personal punishment. Each morning rises, its arms filled with gifts, like an expanse of fresh snow in which we leave our trace and which gives us the illusion of starting over again on a new footing. It suffices to close one's eyes and sleep to be reborn like a new being. This darkness was necessary to allow us to spring up again into the full light of dawn. Bad days pass because, 365 times a year, we have the possibility of getting through them and doing away with them. Contrary to the film *Groundhog Day*,[5] a marvellous fable about love and time, we are not the prisoners of a single cycle of twenty-four hours that repeats itself over and over, every morning. Some days are simple passageways conveying us through the week; others are dungeons from which we have hastened to escape; and still others have the clarity of an open window on the splendor of things.

In this respect, sleep is a marvellous symbol of oblivion and renewal: it offers us the feeling, which may be illusory but is stimulating, of a rebirth after a good night, when we approach the world with rested eyes. It is a miracle to emerge from the darkness, to abandon one's earlier form like a snake shuffling off its old skin to begin a period in which everything seems possible again. The creatures of the night are dissipated, they have returned to their ghostly state. The sweet intoxication of the rising sun, accompanied by birdsong, dazes us. We detach ourselves from the old self to create a new one. *That is the beauty of morning: that of a renewed connection with the world.* It is a sort of psychic passport that we grant ourselves in order to re-enter everyday life. Rising, showering, drinking coffee or tea – these elementary acts re-establish a close solidarity with things, bring us back into the world. To do away with sleep, as some maniacs wish to do because it is a waste of time, would be to kill the power of dreams that blur borderlines, to break with the circadian rhythms and diminish the magic of alternation. Madame de Staël became completely unable to sleep a few weeks before her death, but, even though she was a great devourer of books and ideas, she moaned: "Life is too long without sleep. There isn't enough of interest for twenty-four hours."[6] A single day is therefore all days, from rising to going to bed; a single day is a whole life. Like the hero, according to Nietzsche, we die at dusk every evening and reappear the next day.

The eternal return of good things – for example, the fundamental cultural fact of three daily meals – is in itself a source of pleasure. Time seems to stand still and even to be nullified. In *The Magic Mountain*, Thomas Mann, referring to the sanatorium at Davos, wrote:

> It is always the same day – it just keeps repeating itself. Although since it is always the same day, it is surely not correct to speak of "repetition." One should speak of monotony, of an abiding now, of eternalness. Someone brings you your midday soup, the same soup they brought you yesterday and will bring again tomorrow. And in that moment it comes over you – you don't know how or why, but you feel dizzy watching them bring in the soup. The tenses of verbs become confused, they blend and what is now revealed to you as the true sense of all existence is the "inelastic present," the tense in which they bring you soup for all eternity.[7]

For his part, Paul Morand explained: "On a cruise ship, the first thing that goes overboard is time." The great philosopher Immanuel Kant also experienced a metronomic regularity in Königsberg, in East Prussia, on the shores of the Baltic, rising and going to bed at fixed times, five o'clock in the morning and ten o'clock in the evening, and taking the same, unchanging walk that only two events managed to upset, the reading of Rousseau's *Émile* in 1762 and the announcement of the French Revolution in 1789.

Thus there are privileged places – boarding houses, sanatoriums, barracks, convents and cruise ships – which seem to escape the ebb and flow, as borrowings from a deceptive stability. A beneficial illusion: a life regulated like clockwork produces the feeling of the most perfect immobility. In these radiant cities, you feel sheltered from the tempests of the world. Order and discipline free you from the torment of the passing hours, and boredom is another name for security. By a stupefying paradox, obedience to a timetable sabotages from the inside the experience of time. To kill time, just follow it scrupulously, from second to second. We know about all those people who derive an incredible energy from their allegiance to rules that reassure and guide them. First of all, they organize themselves, construct a schedule, and make a grid of the hours, paying no attention to what they will put into them. Dividing days and weeks into separate compartments is indispensable for them. Their day begins with unshakeable prescriptions analogous to those of a religious liturgy: straightening up the house, arranging items on their desk, putting clothes in a certain order, doing a few calisthenics. The completion of the ritual constitutes their daily prayer. Then Monday, Tuesday, Wednesday lose their specific colors because they are only specimens of the same substance.

In France, haven't we all remained eternal school-children, dividing up the year in accord with the calendar of National Education, All Saint's Day, Christmas, Mardi Gras, Easter? Since 1936, our vacations have been sacred; they connect us with one another, shape a common imagination shared by different generations. Vacations are our national novel, just as work is the backbone of the Americans, the Japanese and the Chinese. Conversely, overwork - that is, the desire to win time back from time – is often a symptom of growing old: we want to combine tasks, urgently hastening to get them done before the end comes, whereas listlessness, that marvellous ability to waste time, that nonchalant stroll through hours and days, is reserved for the young, who have all their years before them. That is their frivolity and their genius.

REASONS TO LIVE

"It is natural," said Thomas Mann, "that a middle-aged man looks upon his period with ill humour." As life grows shorter, some people's disgust with it increases. Because it does them the affront of leaving them, they trample on it. They are going to exit the stage, and they decree that the human adventure is over, their time contemptible, their successors uncultivated and foolish. What kind of world are we going to leave to our children?, asks popular wisdom. "What children are we going to leave to tomorrow's world?", retorts Jaime Semprún. Old age often falls into the double trap of rambling and execration. The grouch, the curmudgeon, the Scrooge lurk within each of us, ready to rail at the slightest disappointment. Montaigne called these maladies "the wrinkles in our minds. ... We never, or rarely, see a soul that in growing old does not come to smell sour and musty."[8]

We must age without allowing our hearts to wither; we must keep an appetite for the world, for pleasures, a curiosity about the generations that will succeed us. In this regard a Schopenhauer or a Cioran, those great slanderers of this world, offer reinvigorating reading insofar as the violence of their arguments against life can be read in their works as a back-handed declaration of love. The sour-tempered person finds no reason for joy: everything dismays him – his friends as well as his close relatives, spring as well as winter or summer. In his eyes, society is ugly, but it is his eyes that are

---

ugly, not the objects he contemplates. He is blanketed by what the philosopher Edmund Husserl called "the ashes of great lassitude." Old people like to think that the world is falling apart because they are going to leave it and don't want to regret it. But it will survive us, and young people laugh at our curses. Prophecies of decline are never more than the application to the history of humanity of the fate reserved for each of us: senescence and death. Old age is, more than any other, the time of *acedia*, that illness that struck Christian ascetics holed up in their solitary retreats, distracting them from the love of God. Instead of burning with ecstasy, they sank into sorrow, lost interest in salvation, and left their cells to return to the frivolous world. The aged person no longer has that resource: he is condemned to trample on his fate with a sort of morose delectation. The fog that corrupts his mind seems to lead only to night. What reasons can we give for living fifty, sixty or seventy years? Exactly the same ones we give for living to twenty, thirty or forty. Existence remains delicious to those who cherish it, odious to those who curse it. And one can pass from one position to the other in a single stretch of time, alternating despair with effusiveness. At any age, life is a permanent battle between fervor and fatigue. The human adventure has no meaning; it is just an absurd and magnificent offering.

> I don't know where I come from
> I don't know who I am
> I don't know when I'll die
> I don't know where I'm going
> I'm amazed to be so merry.
> (Martinus von Biberach, a sixteenth-century German theologian)

The two natures of repetition

If time is a remonstrance, it can also become a recompense when it offers us the illusion, absurd but necessary, of starting a new life every morning. It is simultaneously a countdown that leads us toward the end and the divine permission to make the same mistake over and over. Repetition is an ambivalent power, sterilizing and ferti-lizing; it dries out as much as it transforms. Repeating is the minimal condition for maintaining oneself over time and progressing, whereas the two temporalities that inhabit us, linear flow and the cycle, seem to be recon-ciled and produce the feeling of a progress through an apparent inertia. We don't like repetitions, and yet life consists of nothing else: resuming an athletic activity, an artistic practice or a discipline, re-creating a role in the theatre, taking over a business in difficulty, re-reading a forgotten classic, remarriage, meeting a long-lost friend again, reinserting a past act into the present. Repetition "is a re-collection in advance," said Kierkegaard, a "second power of consciousness,"[9] a positive nostalgia that creates a future. Because it is necessary "to have become familiar with life before beginning to live," repetition exhumes buried aptitudes, awakens unsuspected possibilities. In other words, as in the figure of the spiral, everything returns but never returns the same, and never in the same place: it is an illusion to believe that one becomes a new person, but it is a still more serious illusion to despair of a new blooming. Life has the twofold structure of the same old tune and surprise. Fertile repetition protects us from sterile rambling. It is a source of pleasure when it produces something new under the mask of the déjà vu, dynamiting convention in order to take it elsewhere. False familiarity fabricates strangeness under the pretext of respecting the rules. But the same old tune itself is a complex system; if it overwhelms some, it reassures others and constitutes a psychic shelter where we are protected from the attacks of the world. There is something hypnotic about the hum of an entirely foreseeable existence.

Consider music: in Ravel's *Boléro*, for instance, as Jankélévitch and Clément Rosset have shown, the eternal return of the same theme is a twofold source of joy and tragedy and constitutes this paradox: a stationary progression. The insistent repetition reassures and delights us, the ostinato is innovative. It is said that, until he was ninety-six years old, the great cellist Pablo Casals played the same piece by Bach every day, without ever feeling anything other than a renewed joy.[10] The Orient was able to make reiteration a marvellous artistic motif, by endlessly repeating a single theme. All repetitions are not identical, and they end up producing slight deviations. Consider, for example, the beauty of Umm Kulthum's interminable monotone chants, which seem unchanging to Western ears but constantly introduce small differences in intensity and in intonation that are perceptible to an attentive listener. And the same might be said about the great Indian music that is a petrified movement, an intoxicating dwelling on a note held and modulated indefinitely. The apparent rarity of melody opens the way to subtler sensations than the simple profusion of sound. These microscopic alterations require a different kind of listening.

That is also the object of education: learning by going over the material again and again. We know that only persistence and obstinacy, which are often terribly monotonous, are capable of inculcating a discipline in us and of overcoming difficulties. By repeatedly reviewing our work we finally master it. Likewise, in philosophy, the sciences, politics and economics we have tirelessly to rehash the ideas that are not immediately received or assimilated. For an artist, a leader, a researcher, repeating oneself is a sign not of infirmity but of determination. Great discoveries are made only by indefatigably returning to the same subject, plowing the same furrow. Perseverance is the catechism of will. But there are also culpable obstinacies, like those of former protestors who, as they grow old, fall into *the leftism of andropause*, indulging in the illusion that they have not aged, and adopting, without critical examination, the Maoist or Trotskyist slogans of their youth. They call fidelity what is no more than a pig-headed persistence in stupidity.

Repetition creates divergence on the basis of redundancy. Consider traditional clocks and watches: they produce rectilinearity out of a circumference and are truly "a moving image of eternity" (Plato).[11] The hands of a watch, focused on the fine tatting of the hours and seconds, can rotate on and on, like a hamster in its wheel, producing the illusion that nothing changes, that time moves on pitilessly, and that day will soon have disappeared at midnight. "[C]an you travel great distances without getting anywhere? ... If you travel in circles."[12] The watch, a geometric site of the junction of time and eternity, is unique in that it is a voluntary deception: a perfect sphere, it gives, contrary to the hour glass, the impression that nothing is moving, that everything is reproduced without drama. The watch hand, the strait gate between the past and the future, describes in its gyration a false stagnation. It is a round dance that pretends to remain in place. Here we are far from the utopia of Nietzsche's eternal return, where the "house of being" is rebuilt in identical form and for always, year after year. Repetition, on the contrary, is a reiteration that inaugurates, that invents.

In a brilliantly provocative story, Borges imagines that a man named Pierre Menard, copying at the beginning of the twentieth century, line for line and word for word, a few pages of Cervantes' *Don Quixote*, produces an absolutely new text that is rich with all the centuries that have elapsed in the meantime, and far more subtle than the original.[13] These two prose works, similar in appearance, are therefore entirely different. The Same is no more than a masked Other; fellow humans resemble each other in no way. This Borgesian sophism makes us dizzy. It dismantles all notions of intellectual property and copying: if we accept it, we can stipulate that an author who re-created today, word for word, all the great classics of the Western canon could not be suspected of plagiarism. The copy would be a re-creation, perhaps even superior to the original works. Duplication would constitute a tremendous achievement. To repeat or imitate would then be to diverge completely ...

The eternal rebirth

What remains to be done when we think we've seen everything, experienced everything? Constantly beginning over, because time allows us to reiterate as often as we want. The flesh is not sad, thank God, and we will never have read all the books.[14] Life goes on: that frightfully simple sentence is perhaps the secret of a happy longevity. Real life is not heroic or extravagant; it is first of all down to earth, in the felt and quenched thirst, shared everyday life. We consist of "little todays," to quote one of Romain Gary's characters. Therefore we must begin by persisting, refusing to slow down, disengage, yield. Act as if we were going to last for decades, continue to look to the future, to project. "I'm running toward my death," said the Italian philosopher Norberto Bobbio (1909–2004), "and where I stop running, there is my death."

Hence living consists in transforming an accident into a choice in order to constitute a destiny – but a pliable destiny that remains flexible to the end. Time may lead us toward a gradual decline, but it also never ceases to offer us another chance – that is the good news. It is not a wheel that inexorably breaks our bones; it is a series of bifurcations, intersections that offer an opportunity to rectify what we did wrong the first time. It justifies those who keep trying when they are granted a second, third or fourth chance. "I would like to be able never to stop coming into the world," said J.-B. Pontalis magnificently. This rebirth is no more miraculous than that of the insects, mentioned by David Henry Thoreau, whose larvae, enclosed in the solid wood of a table, were awakened by the warmth of a teapot.[15] Right to the end, we remain merely sketched out, and we leave unfinished. Not only, following a romantic encounter, may there be a discovery, a journey or a sudden rejuvenation, what in France used to be called "St Martin's summer,"[16] but in life there are late departures that harbor a whole layer of possible destinies.

If there is a nation that has based its credo on eternally beginning again, at the risk of making it a myth, it is surely the United States of America, since there each generation starts over on new bases, erases the liabilities of the earlier ones, and redefines the social contract. We are always living on a trial basis; *existence is above all an experiment.* It is less a straight line that tends toward a goal than a shortcut that advances along indirect avenues and collects in its rings all its earlier cycles. Thus we traverse several lives of unequal duration and density. If, as Plato said, "the beginning is a god who, as long as he remains among humans, saves everything," beginning over is a second breath that elevates minds and protects them from petrification, from despondency. That is what leads the mountain climber to find a new burst of energy

when he is on the brink of exhaustion, what incites
discouraged students or researchers to persevere in their
efforts, activists to continue the battle against injustice, and
entrepreneurs to overcome obstacles. Apart from birth,
there are few absolute origins in a human life, but there
are innumerable rebirths, turns, slippages.[17] They are our
safe-conduct passes, the permission accorded everyone to
grope his way forward, to go astray, to start again. Each
fiasco is a springboard for a new attempt. A happy life is
like the phoenix, setting itself against itself, consuming
the form it has given itself, rising from its former ashes to
recycle itself endlessly.

The fact that after a certain age life becomes more
foreseeable does not make it less intriguing. Reliving
something is as exciting as discovering it for the first time,
and the fact that sensations have already been felt changes
nothing. In adolescence, we sometimes dream of a second
birth in which we would no longer owe anything to our
parents and would be our own origins. In that sense, Indian
summer is a little like a repetition of the teenage dilemma.
The goal is to find again within us the faith that creates, the
power that invents, the giddiness that hesitates faced with
the abundance of possible paths. Twilight must resemble
dawn, even if dawn will not open onto any new day.

Swan song or dawn?

An eternal question for each of us: how can we transform
into a creative power the destructive element in passing
time? In the pictorial or literary domain, some people,
especially the greatest artists, have prodigious old ages,
when they reach their fullest development. To the myth
of Rimbaud, of the child poet who burns out at the age

of twenty, we should oppose the reality of a creation that culminates over time. That is what Baudelaire observed apropos of Goya. At the end of his career, Goya's eyes were so weak, it is said, that someone had to sharpen his pencils for him.

> And yet he made, at that period in his life, very important large lithographs, admirable engravings, vast tableaux in miniature – further proof of the singular law that presides over the destiny of great artists and that insists that since life is governed contrary to intelligence, they gain in one respect what they lose in the other, and that they thus continue, following a progressive youth, to grow stronger, more energetic, and more audacious, right up to the edge of the grave.[18]

About Beethoven, Nietzsche said that he was "the intermediate event between an old mellow soul that is constantly breaking down, and a future over-young soul that is always coming; there is spread over his music the twilight of eternal loss and eternal extravagant hope ..."[19] Beethoven's swan song is simultaneously an overture. It is impossible to decide whether the apparent desiccation of the late works marks the exhaustion of his inspiration or a spurt of creativity. The American sociologist David Riesman also noted this phenomenon: "Some individuals bear within them the sources of their own renewal; growing old increases their wisdom without depriving them of their spontaneity or their ability to enjoy life ... as long as their bodies do not turn into an active enemy, these men are immortal because of their aptitude for renewing themselves."[20]

How can this fail to remind us of the use by the French writer Romain Gary at the end of his life of the pseudonym "Émile Ajar," which allowed him to twin himself in two completely distinct authors, one serious and almost tragic and the other burlesque and funny, in order to publish nine books in six years under one name or the other, maintaining the mystery of this deception until he died? A perfect example of rebirth on the part of a writer who feared sinking into the common crowd.[21] Ageing creators appear, in their last works, not as exhausted artists but as demiurges ahead of their time: for example, *Falstaff*, Verdi's last opera, where *bel canto* is abandoned in favor of a total flexibility and liberty, or Chateaubriand's *La Vie de Rancé*, which Julien Gracq analyzed in these terms: "The language of *La Vie de Rancé* drives a more mysterious point toward the future: his messages in code, staccato, out of step, which break up the narrative, out of the blue, as if they were picked up from another planet, already stammer news of the country where Rimbaud is going to awaken."[22] The German composer Wolfgang Rihm maintains that "art has no age": "When I compose, I even regress in biological time. Sometimes I'm 89 years old, then 4, then 53, then 26½ then 73, until I am dead – that is, I correspond provisionally to the clichés of art. Of course, I will never be adult, that's part of the game."[23] Thus in the land of creation, but also in the most trivial everyday life, comings and goings are multiple: childhood and adolescence last, as least as potentiality, until an advanced time. Up to a certain point, we can turn time like a spoon, in all directions.

AGES IN CONFLICT

Each generation enters active life convinced that it will do better than the preceding ones, and it considers the latter with disdain or anger. Parents and teachers appear as encumbering vestiges, old people who have to be pushed aside to clear the way. Young people are impatient to steal a march on them, and forthwith. Conversely, adults see the newcomers as little savages who can't be taught anything. They want to erase us, they say; let them just try to equal us! There are decisive generations and neutral generations. In France, the generation of World War II, the Algerian War and May 1968, the generation of anti-totalitarianism, put their stamp, in one way or another, on their time. The truth that each of them bears is contested; young people are tempted to sweep them away because they can blame on them everything that is going badly. They can also envy their elders ("I would really have liked to have lived during the Resistance, or to be able to remake the world in the 1970s") and accuse them of having betrayed their ideals. Some generations make history, while others make commentaries and claim to rekindle the flame abandoned by their great ancestors: for example, when minority groups today attempt a grotesque return to the utopias of the Bolsheviks or Fidel Castro. Karl Marx: "All great world-historical facts and personages appear, so to speak, twice ... the first time as tragedy, the second time as farce."[24] These critical moments ricochet off one another like the aftershocks of an earthquake: May 1968, which was itself a parody, a stage prop room from 1917, Cuba and Maoist China, is being aped in turn by a whole group of young people who want to commit to something. The "Yellow Vests" in Paris in 2018 and 2019 have vaguely imitated the French Revolution with cardboard guillotines to decapitate President Emmanuel Macron. "Empty periods," Sartre opined, "are those that choose to see themselves with eyes that have already been invented. They can do nothing but refine discoveries made by others, because the person who provides the eye also provides the thing seen."[25] The term "generation" is itself problematic: we are not supportive or close to people of our own age because we share a date of birth with them. It is only on the basis of experience that we are affiliated with that precise group. The older we get, the more we are amalgamated, wrongly, with our biological contemporaries, forcibly caught up with them in the nets of a single temporal compartment. But our minds, our tastes, carry us elsewhere. As if all newborns in a maternity ward were doomed to develop together from birth to death, bound to one another by the accident of a number and an hour.

Every parent and every educator delivers two kinds of teaching. The first is official and consists of a set of principles and values that he proclaims overtly and defends. The second is involuntary, and he transmits it unconsciously, through his attitude and his relations with others, and it may be diametrically opposed to what he professes. Sometimes his offspring instantly copy the tacit behaviors, through a subterranean imitation, and neglect the explicit message, regarding it as mere clutter. We also convey, whether we want to or not, a resemblance with our parents. As we grow old, we can become similar to the father we hated or the mother we found ridiculous and odious. Their quirks rub off on us; we adopt their tics and use their expressions. They may also imprint themselves physically on us, invade our face, superimpose their features on our own. We are marked, regardless of our wishes, and all the more because we reject the legacy. Every child grows up on the symbolic erasure of his parents. He will twist their teachings or, worse yet, forget them. In his turn, he will love, suffer in his own way, and communicate his neuroses or illusions to his offspring – who will contest them.

It is often said that young people no longer respect us. But we are hurt if they insist on calling us Mr and Mrs when we address them with their first names. And if they stand up to give us their seat in the bus, it's even worse. That means that we have passed over to the other side. They establish distance where we sought closeness. They put us in our place. Sometimes sons and daughters, after rebelling against their elders, are reconciled with them late in life. They toe the line after sowing their wild oats; their critical eye has enriched their view of the world, and this detour was necessary before they could ultimately rejoin the great temporal chain and become a single link in a lineage that transcends them. The mysterious path of continuity is followed through the apparent rejection of that lineage. The negation of the heritage was its secret prolongation.

CHAPTER 4

The Interweaving of Time

If every man couldn't live many different
lives, he couldn't live his own, either.

PAUL VALÉRY

Even a loaded life might be easier when
one had added a new necessity to it.

HENRY JAMES[1]

Confronted by time that makes us and unmakes us, we
have at least two strategies at our disposal: enjoying the
present moment or not worrying about the length of our
lives. This double postulate was defended by the Ancients,
who issued two contradictory commandments: live as if
you were to die at any moment and live as if you were
never going to die. Seneca, following Marcus Aurelius and
Epictetus, urged us to experience each day as if it were the
last, calling on the soul to "present its accounts," while at
the same time thanking the gods for granting us one more

day. Long before them, Aristotle assigned a noble mission to humans: to become immortal, they had to give priority to the life of the mind, the contemplative life (*theoria*), which alone allows us to achieve an almost divine wisdom, and to avoid limiting their thoughts to material things alone.[2]

Let's examine the first position: "What makes a way of life perfect is to live each day as if it were the last," said the Stoics. The observation is noble but difficult to put into practice, except for someone who is sentenced to die and is awaiting execution, an elderly, very ill person who is subject to the vicissitudes of his health, or a political prisoner: "Foreseeing one's life a day in advance made no sense," said the Russian writer Varlam Shalamov (1907–1982), who was to spend twenty years of his life in a Gulag. But no one could sleep peacefully if each night he feared he would die in his sleep. Here we are confronted by a dogma of brevity that cannot stand up to lived experience. There is no possible joy without a minimum of optimism about time, without a belief that the coming weeks might improve matters. Thinking every night that the last day has just passed, slipping into one's bed as if it were a shroud, is untenably pretentious.

Live as if you were to die at any moment?

"Consider every day as a completed life."[3] So commands prudence, as much as it invites us to multiply our pleasures. We must live and see the world as if for the first time, live and see it as if for the last time. In one case, look upon it with new eyes; in the other, enjoy existing as something good that can be taken away from us in an instant. We concentrate on the moment for fear that it will never return.

It is a flash of light and a fragment stolen from time. Thus in living well there are, at every age, two complementary proposals: that of carpe diem, the art of seizing the day, the hour, the occasion, and that of the project, the long time whose end we cannot imagine. Each moment is definitive, each moment is a transition. Nonetheless, the idea that each morning is our last can spoil every pleasure. A pleasure, a love affair, a friendship are valuable only if they open the prospect of a common future. "To philosophize is to learn to die," said Montaigne, borrowing from Plato. It is already sad enough that we must die. If in addition we have to be obsessed from morning to night with that fatal event, there is no point in coming into the world. So one would be supposed to practice dying all through one's life to avoid being surprised when the Grim Reaper arrives, or to meditate on a skull, as the great Christians did in the face of the Vanities. Isn't that the best way to ruin life by subjecting it to the daily guillotine of its end, to the *memento mori*?[4]

"The present alone is our happiness," according to Diogenes; and it is so because it has a tomorrow and is not squeezed in the infernal grip of the now and the later. That is a philosophically seductive position, but it is existentially untenable. So we have to invert it: to philosophize is to learn to live, and especially to re-live, within the horizon of finitude. Each day, as we have seen, is a metaphor of existence, with its triumphal morning, its radiant noon and its calm evening, even if each life has the structure of a year, with its spring, its radiant summer, its autumn and its winter. And yet we wake up the next day, and we celebrate the new year.

What about the individuals who recommended this kind of asceticism? For the record, Seneca died at sixty-one, forced to commit suicide by Nero after making shady compromises with the masters of the empire; Marcus

Aurelius died at fifty-eight, poisoned in Vienna on the orders of his son Commodius; and Epictetus died at seventy-five or eighty, depending on the biographer. Thus they had ample time to consider the future, and Marcus Aurelius had time to shape the destiny of the Roman Empire. Let us repeat: one of the conditions of pleasure is that it be infinitely reproducible. Each instant of happiness wants its return, its expansion, its Encore. That is the promise of time, and every promise bears within it a certain lack of moderation: it commits beyond its possibilities, it madly postulates a future. So long as we feed on that illusion, hope dominates experience. Even a centenarian makes plans and talks about tomorrow.

The old boudoir of the past

What is true of individuals is true for peoples, Proust said; there is something worse than plagiarism, and that is self-plagiarism[5] – imitating oneself while thinking that one is inventing something new. But the claim is not entirely pertinent. We often innovate only by aping ourselves, just as Proust himself never ceased to plumb his genius by copying and recopying himself until he had found his own voice. We mechanically recite formulas learned by heart until, from these litanies, a spark is kindled. Self-creation or re-creation always springs from the struggle between an imitated form and a new form that is trying to emerge. We begin by yielding to automatic reflexes, by reproducing the usual behaviors, before we alter them, just a little.

To make progress, one has to know how to regress. Educating a child always involves retreats that are not failures but ways of moving backward to prepare a new advance: undoing a behavior in order to reorganize it in a different way. The virtues of a certain regression are the same at every age. All the cold pasts we leave behind us are never completely extinguished. Faulkner's famous phrase, repeated *ad nauseam*, to the effect that "the past is never dead. It's not even past," is generally interpreted as a tragedy, proof that the weight of earlier tragedies continues to hinder us. However, it can also be understood in a less sombre sense as a call to delve into our lived experience, as if it were a cavern into which we descend, like speleologists, to awaken buried periods and transform memory into future. All our selves sketched out or unfinished, those that dream of a great career or a fabulous destiny converge once again; energies are reawakened like extinct volcanos. We have to give up some ambitions; they either get us going again or are replaced by others. To live a long time is never to finish mourning for our past aspirations. "I have great, unsatisfied departures in me," said Gabriel Fauré. A virtuality prematurely repressed – for example, the dream of a career – is revived: these spectres inhabit us like possibilities incubating as they wait to hatch. Not to mention the imaginary exploits on which we pride ourselves – acts of heroism, poignant romances that are unverifiable because no one is still there to contradict us. We need these fabulous legends to support the dreadful platitude of our days, and with time we end up believing our own fictions and lying with complete sincerity.

The past is not only a worm-eaten cadaver. At the same time, it is "a large chest of drawers stuffed with balance sheets," an "old boudoir full of withered roses" (Baudelaire) that intimidates us; but it is also a chiffonier holding dormant marvels, magical spells temporarily dozing. If it still mutters in our consciousness, that proves that it wants to assert itself and shake up mummified life. All through the years we experience different versions of ourselves that we hold concurrently as we shed our preceding selves. We shelter tactless or furious lodgers who demand repairs or just want to elbow one another. Even in grown-ups, there is always a mischievous child who wants to reappear, an abandoned being that demands consolation, a frustrated vocation that re-emerges. Everyone is an unsatisfied, loquacious multitude. Dead memories, as Proust taught us, ask only to be brought back to life. Revisiting our own history can have therapeutic virtues, and especially fanciful ones. We suspect that, as we move forward, something essential has been lost and that it is important to find it again. Some people pile up newspapers, letters or knick-knacks as relics of a time that they wish to preserve from the dark night of oblivion, at the cost of transforming themselves into guards in the museum of their lives or visitors to a cemetery. Others do the opposite, looking at themselves in the distorting mirror of retrospection in order to make a new start.

THE ART OF NOT BEING JUST GRANDPARENTS

We can rejoice in having grandchildren someday and defining, like Victor Hugo, *The Art of Being a Grandfather*,[6] as "the art of being children," of being benevolent tutelary figures who offer advice more than they issue orders, situating themselves in a lineage by discerning a similarity just below the surface of the newcomer's face. Then we enjoy all the advantages of the kids without the inherent servitudes. With them, we learn again life's first faltering steps, the pleasures of the report cards that we compare with our own, half a century earlier, and we marvel on seeing them grow and become brilliant students, dare to do what we ourselves failed to do, take the family in a new direction. They don't constantly judge us, don't take revenge, are not machines generating accusations. Even their caprices are delicious, because they are temporary, and their childish remarks enchant us, even the silliest of them; they allow tenderness without the tension.

However, this affectionate authority does not exhaust either the life or the still abundant energy of a man or a woman of sixty or seventy. Especially since the latter, in a sort of reverse transmission, have to obey the orders of their own sons and daughters, who know better what is good for their offspring. Grandparents are allowed to care for the little ones but on conditions set by their young parents, who are scandalized to see their fathers and mothers use an overloaded schedule as an excuse for not taking the children on the dates requested or for not picking them up after school. Instead of being available 24/7, now the grandfather or grandmother, who are often separated or remarried, have their own lives, leave on trips, attend university classes, go out on the town! Then they no longer want to be called grandpa and grandma, those terrible names that smell musty and send you directly to the cemetery. "Papa" and "Mama" are hardly better, so we try to find other pet names, forging more or less poetic neologisms. In short, the function vacillates, but it hasn't disappeared; if only for economic reasons, it has ceased to be immutable. Getting old does not mean only being babysitters or sharing memories recited melancholically; instead, it means traversing common battles, defining objectives, fighting for projects. Being grandparents is no longer an identity, it is just an additional, exciting stage in life.

It's always the first time

We live in the fog of the present, without always understanding what is happening to us. Some events become comprehensible to us only long afterward. We decipher them in the half-light of a wobbly but belated memory. The alien nature of our past is not only a dispossession, but also a way of enjoying oneself a posteriori, when reminiscence becomes revival. We didn't realize how complex, how profuse we were! New possibilities can emerge from the mass of memories like doves that a magician pulls out of his hat. Predicting the future is difficult, but it is even harder to predict the past, which constantly changes as the days go by and which we tint with various affects as it comes back to us. Whence the temporal paradoxes of which novelists are so fond; we are nostalgic for the future and prophetic about yesteryear, which never ceases to irrupt violently in our present, to engage in an unprecedented colloquy.

In other words, life moves both forward and backward. The tragedy of old age, Mauriac said, is that it is the sum total of a life, a sum in which we cannot change a single figure.[7] It is supposed to be irremediable. But this sum total is friable and constantly being recomposed like a mobile mosaic. The possible weariness of the already experienced, that immense "What's the point?" that lies in wait for us, from adolescence on, is eliminated by a kind of amnesia regarding pleasures. We always enjoy for the first time, no matter how sharp our recollections, which carry the long genealogy of past delights. Where the pleasures of love or food are concerned, the past functions as a stimulus: it educates our senses, our intelligence and our taste buds instead of anesthetizing them. It carries along with it a whole layer of old bedazzlements that are added to the present ones. The diffraction of flavors in gastronomy, for instance, or the thrills of orgasm are in no way diminished by having been preceded by others. If I have never eaten such tender meat, never felt such a powerful orgasm, that is because my body is paying homage to a long life of epicureanism while at the same time asserting the pre-eminence of the present moment. Both our skin and our senses are freighted with a history that is as opulent as it is discreet. Our artistic taste is rich with all the works we have experienced, which, far from making us blasé, prepare us for new musical or pictorial impacts. There is a discontinuous amnesia that reminds us of its existence the better to erase itself. Past stirrings never drain off the power of current sensations. We wouldn't take so much pleasure in eating if we had to remember with sorrow that we had already eaten the day before. We always sit down to eat hungry, and happily greedy; and we don't care at all about our last meal. The delight of the dish is rekindled by the memory of past delectations that refine it. Forgetting is the precondition for enjoyment thanks to the marvellous erasing machine that is the human brain.

Become like children again?

So life is a river that sometimes comes back to its source when the inversion of time's trajectories is practiced: first growing old, then getting younger as one ages. The world is ancient, Hannah Arendt said, and the child enters it to revolutionize it like a ferment.[8] But sometimes a person's mature age is renewed by a childhood that grows within him as he moves away from it: childhood not as a reality but as a mental disposition. Living well consists in dying and awakening, in a series of alternations, right to the end.

This is the religious phenomenon of the Revival, a recovery of faith in which beliefs acquire renewed vitality. It also applies to musical genres, singers (or politicians) who were thought to have disappeared but who suddenly re-emerge and attract fervent crowds again. "Has-beens" sometimes return to grace, and the "comeback kid" is the very paradigm of modernity: on the dial of the media's lottery, there is always a compartment for former stars, abandoned singers, underestimated writers. Fortune is a good mother: she sometimes plucks the forgotten from oblivion and, throwing them once again into the public spotlight, feeds them to the hungry crowds.

Thus it is a question of rediscovering the childlike (and not the childish) – that is, the spirit of revelation. "How great man would be metaphysically if the child was his teacher,"[9] wrote Gaston Bachelard, commenting on Søren Kierkegaard. "We have such an urgent need to learn from a life that is beginning, from a soul that is blossoming, from a mind that is opening."[10] What does it mean to learn from childhood? First of all, to realize that at sixty, even seventy, despite our experience, we are just as lost as we were at twenty, minus the hope of being able to put things right. We have washed up, naked, on the shores of time, like old kids who have to reinvent a virginal perception of the world, a disposition to be surprised. In a certain way, we long for the blessed ignorance of children, which seems so rich with a fundamental intuition, rather than the semi-darkness of the adult whose head is stuffed with useless knowledge. Nothing is more admirable, but also more sterile, sometimes, than the knowledge accumulated over the years, the empty erudition that splits hairs, quibbles over a word or a figure because it has lost sight of the whole. What luck to still be able to discover for the first time the classics, great music, major films, to examine the world with absolutely new eyes! After a certain age, the only youth that awaits us is not that of the body, as in the Faust myth, but that of the intelligence and emotion.

No one will grow younger, but it remains possible to enrich our consciousness, to maintain the spirit of exploration and observation, despite the passing years: these are two antagonistic kinds of growth that compete but do not cancel each other out, establishing a beneficial tension in each of us. The fall into vulnerability does not alter the depth of thought, which follows its own trajectory. St Francis asked that we remain close to our first years, and that we break the limits of the old self by immersing it in the purifying bath of childhood. To age without allowing one's heart to grow old, keeping a taste for the world, for pleasures, is to avoid the twofold trap of anxious introspection and disgust. There are at least two childhoods in a life, and this is true at every age: the first that leaves us at puberty and another that survives when we are adults, enlightening us by ardent visitations and escaping us as soon as we try to capture or imitate it. The re-descent into childhood is not a descent into puerility but, rather, a rejuvenating innocence of the mind, a beneficial rupture that irrigates us with new blood. It is therefore a way of putting oneself in a posture of astonishment, opposed to a petrified and fossilized life: a capacity for reconciling intelligence and the sensible, of welcoming the unknown. At every age, the ability to bounce back can win out over the concern for self-preservation and the laziness of the status quo. "Life is like playing a violin solo in public and learning the instrument as one goes on," said Samuel Butler (1835–1902). Until our last day, we never cease to practice our scales, to play the notes awkwardly. We're all invalid, sick, broken, quibbling, stupid old men and women, hence sure to have a great future. Then childhood is no longer a pathetic travesty into which the withered adult falls but the joyous supplement of someone who wants to immerse him- or herself in the charm of the first years. It marks the septuagenarian's face the way precocious senility sometimes marks a young person's face, since stupidity, as we know, may appear before we are old.

Our phantom selves

Thus we all enter into dialogue with the diverse generations that compose us – the child that we were, the adult that we are, and the old people that we will become – to bring them back to life or to ward them off. What is the status of these avatars? Are they ghosts, anticipations or revenants? Ever since the Middle Ages, a ghost has been an anonymous dead person whom we meet by chance, whereas the revenant is a dead person close to the living.[11] But sometimes the kid or the adolescent that we were has become as distant from us as a stranger, and their emergence is less a return than an apparition. So long as the conversation between these diverse periods is maintained, life retains its minimum level. Each person remains a confluence of several voices that argue, agree and separate, accumulating discords and wonders, tenacity and candor. (An anthropologist tells us that, among the Bambara, a Manding-speaking people in Mali, a special rejuvenation rite allows old men to become seven-year-old children and women to become virgins again.)[12] Age is no more than an indicator from which we can automatically deduce a style, a way of being. The secret of a happy maturity is first of all indifference toward maturity qua summons. Gradual decay goes hand in hand with redemption; at every moment we want to remain wise men and madmen, reasonable and mischievous, prudent and bold. What maturity envies in youth, and justly so, is not only its energy, its beauty, its taste for risk, its cognitive plasticity, its way of being reborn to itself, brand new, every morning, but also to have so many things to learn, to discover, so many lives to live, so many passions to feel. This appetite has to be preserved until the end, even at the price of a certain naïveté. *A great lesson of the passing years: we have to start over from zero at any time.* As if we didn't know anything. As if we could finally open up to what had escaped or intimidated us.

Some kinds of belated maturity take fifty or sixty years to appear: "Your fruit is ripe but you aren't ripe for your fruit" (Nietzsche). For his part, Kant maintained that about sixty years were necessary to make a philosopher; before that age, one couldn't write anything original in that domain. Senescence is a compaction of ages; it keeps them all together, for better and for worse. In his diary, the literary critic Matthieu Galey (1934–1986) speaks of the "juvenilo-senile extravagance" of Louis Aragon; after the death of his wife, Elsa Triolet, the communist poet finally acknowledged his homosexuality, appearing in public with young men and crossing Saint-Germain-des-Prés wearing a white mask.[13] Physical decline can cohabit with genius, illnesses with an exceptional acuteness. "Intellectual sight begins to be keen when the visual is entering on its wane,"[14] said Plato. It is the half-light that makes it possible to see, not bright light, which blinds us, especially when we are novices and drawn to sharp contrasts: youth is the magnificent age of the absolute – that is, of heroic vigor – but it is also often the age of crime and stupidity. Only years bring us the art of nuance. Even if there are many senile, raving old people, there are also famous men and women, expert in discernment, who continue to be clear-sighted until a great age and whose intellectual vitality astounds us.

All these incomplete lives that we bear within us, entwined with one another like an umbilicus with a complex script, may sometimes emerge and give rise to an unprecedented temporal current; an ancient fragment returns and becomes a new beginning, flows criss-cross in every direction. *Life is written in tiny letters, but it is a long letter*: the crossing was sometimes perilous, but it was magnificent. The French thinker Pierre Bayle, who advocated tolerance before Voltaire did, asserted the "rights of the errant consciousness," the right to make mistakes, to change one's mind without being forced to embrace a certain truth, a certain religion. In that respect we are errant souls improvising our everyday life day by day. We make our way leisurely toward the end, frequently going astray and narrowly escaping disaster. We have to hurtle down the slope of life as we ascend it.

FISSURES, CRACKS, FRACTURES

"Of course, all life is a process of breaking down, but the blows that do the dramatic side of the work ... don't show their effect all at once. There is another sort of blow that comes from within – that you don't feel until it's too late to do anything about it."[15] Who doesn't know this sumptuous work? The crack-up mentioned by the author of Gatsby is one of those initially invisible fissures that craze blocks of stone and end up fracturing them. Alcohol, romantic disappointments, impoverishment, the loss of illusions and health, the drying up of inspiration, and literary failures give this story a kind of tragic magnificence. In the excellent commentary that he wrote on it, the philosopher Gilles Deleuze starts out from the obvious fact of this short masterpiece, which imposes itself on us with "the sound of a hammer-blow:"[16] life is a battle beyond our strength, from which we emerge broken, as if a crack had constantly widened in us since our birth, making us like those fragile porcelains that break at the slightest shock. Fitzgerald's story is beautiful and irrefutable, like misfortune.

Let us register a protest in accord with a different logic: life is not all destruction and madness, and our freedom also allows us to slow the disintegration. We do not all age at the same speed, and we even have a certain power over death, thanks to suicide. There is no need to invoke, as Deleuze does, the spirits of Antonin Artaud, Malcolm Lowry and Nietzsche in order to rise to the level of these great authors and choose "rather death than the health that we are offered."[17] Here there is a whole conventional fatalism.

The structuralist school of "French theory" remains marked, as does the situationism of a writer such as Guy Debord, by a gloomy romanticism that delights in broken destinies: cleverly, it transforms physical decline into superior intelligence, reinvents Plato's view of the body as an obstacle to truth and health. Since we are mortal, we may as well summon the Grim Reaper as early as possible and destroy ourselves in a fireworks show of pompous phrases. Artistic life inspires two views of the ages: one sombre and tragic, linking intensity with decline, the other luminous and positive, which makes it possible to combine, right to the end, creation and senescence, and of which Picasso or Miró are the best illustrations.

Absurdly perched on the last stages of life without being able to climb down again, we have no choice but to go on, step after step. Although life has often been compared to a ladder, we realize, as we climb the last rungs, that the ladder is not leaning on any wall but instead rests on the void. Like the characters in cartoons who jump off a cliff and continue to pedal with their feet above the abyss, we have to continue to climb as if the ascent would never end.

PART III

Late Love Affairs

5

Desire Late in Life

Montand and I are the same age. While he has
experienced my getting old at his side, I have experienced
his maturation at my side. That's what people say about
men. They mature: gray locks are called "silvery temples."
Wrinkles chisel them, whereas they make women ugly.

SIMONE SIGNORET

I am a repugnant being covered with wrinkles. At night,
before going to bed, when I look at myself in the mirror,
without my dentures, I think have a funny-looking face. My
jawbone doesn't have a single one of my own teeth, either
upper or lower. Moreover, I no longer have even gums. ... I
myself can't get over it. No human being, not even an ape,
would want to have such a hideous face. Obviously, under
such conditions I'm not so stupid as to want to be loved
by women. And instead of the aforementioned aptitudes, I
can push this pretty woman into the arms of a handsome
man, thus provoking a domestic war ... and take pleasure
in that ...[1]

An old man of seventy-three becomes infatuated with his daughter-in-law Sitsuke, a former music-hall dancer who exercises an absolute power over him. Obsessed by the fair sex, although he is impotent, he continues to feel "sexual attraction in accord with various atypical and indirect modalities." In a diary that takes the form of a medical report that considers blood pressure, cardiac rhythm, diet and the paralysis of certain limbs, the Japanese writer Junichirō Tanizaki (1886–1965) shows us the young woman's growing ascendancy over her father-in-law. The whole narrative is tensely strung between two extremes: the narrator's physical degradation and his desire for Sitsuke, whom he bribes with money and gifts. But the rewards are slim: she allows him only little intimacies – seeing her nude in the shower or massaging the sole of her foot. She slaps him as soon as he tries to embrace her and cries: "What a scoundrel this grandfather is!"[2] If he tries to steal a kiss "on the fleshy part of her right shoulder,"[3] he gets another slap on the left cheek. However, she continues to entice him by allowing him to kiss the arch of her foot. "When you touch me, I have to rinse off immediately, otherwise I would feel dirty." She finally concedes him the right to lick her feet passionately in exchange for the gift of a cat's eye gem worth 3 million yen[4] that she covets.

Every time his efforts succeed, he is divided between elation and terror and suffers from little cardiac troubles. Although she is married to the old man's son, Sitsuke takes a lover, a man with whom her admirer is acquainted. He approves of their affair and protects it, without his own family knowing it. She goes so far as to rub her cheek on a dog to make him jealous and watches, amused, his reactions. He puts up with everything, ready to die for a favor, and totally absorbed in his "vile fascination" with this woman who scorns and exploits him. The uglier and more repulsive he finds himself, the more he finds her superior, and the more odious he is toward his wife and children, for whom he wishes nothing but misfortune and misery. Finally, he has his idol's feet cast in bronze to serve as an ornament on his tomb, so that she can forever trample on the bones of the imbecilic old man he has become ...

The graybeard scorned by the lady's maid he is courting, the grandfather ridiculed by the actress or courtesan, the stuck-up old bat infatuated with a young man who mocks her, the elders in the Bible (Book of Daniel, chapter 13) who find the young Susannah taking her bath, try to rape her, and then accuse her of adultery; from Molière to Tennessee Williams, the theatre, literature and, later on, film cruelly present the gap between the suitors, whether men or women, and those they pine for. Toward the end of his life, Chateaubriand fell in love with a young woman who rejected him; Casanova, in a novel by Arthur Schnitzler, was forced when very old to disguise himself as a young lovebird, at night, to seduce a girl. Again, we find Goethe at seventy-two asking, in Marienbad and through the intercession of Grand Duke Karl August of Weimar, for the hand of a quasi-adolescent of nineteen, Ulrike von Levetzow, who declines; Mrs Stone, an American in her fifties, in Rome, in love with the handsome Paolo, who is hardly twenty, and whom she pays, humiliating herself day after day as she watches her life collapsing "in disorderly folds like a tent whose central pole has been taken away."[5] Julie de Lespinasse (1732–1776), a friend of D'Alembert, who fell, at the age of forty, for a younger man, Colonel Guibert, smug and insignificant, whose indifference ended up killing her. Today we see mature women, British, French, German, Canadian or Austrian, going to Cuba, Kenya or Haiti to enjoy themselves by finding robust lovers from whom they demand vigor and feelings.[6] Everywhere, nature seems to be taking revenge for generational misalliances. The mockery is universal and also bears on women who want to continue to be attractive despite their faded charms: from Goya's toothless coquette, already a death's head wearing make-up who hasn't noticed the passing years, to Maupassant's once celebrated actress, from whom "a kind of false youth emanated like a rancid perfume of love," not to forget "the bag of bones with fetid breath" that Théophile de Viau ridiculed in the seventeenth century. Public opinion is cruel to men and women who forget the restraint suited to old age. Only Victor Hugo, in "Booz endormi," imagines an ancestor who has a triumphal night and engenders a child thanks to the caresses of a young woman. But poetry enjoys all the rights that reality denies it.

Asymmetries and expiry dates

In a diary novel written in 1983, Doris Lessing narrates the misadventures of a woman in her forties living in Britain: "One day I stopped at a service station. I'd driven a long time, I was tired, and I said: 'Fill me up.' The attendant replied: 'With pleasure, Madame, but only the tank.'"[7] The novelist Annie Ernaux, relating an episode in which she was the victim of a pickpocket in a department store in Paris when she was forty-five, tells only how, vaguely attracted by the thief's bad-boy looks, she felt "humiliated even more by the fact that so much skill, cleverness and desire was directed to my handbag and not to my body."[8] The philosopher Monique Canto-Sperber sums it up: "Why is it so hard for a middle-aged woman to remake her life?"[9]

Here is the problem, put bluntly: the art of loving and conjugal life are thought to be inaccessible to women beyond a certain threshold. Common opinion does not allow for catch-up sessions for them: in their case, the birthdate is less important than the expiry date. Many people denounce this asymmetry that sees decrepit old men getting involved with young things while women of their age are no longer anything but "old witches"[10] fit for the trash heap, "perishable goods" (Susan Sontag). Men are supposed to get more handsome, women to get uglier. "Ordinary mortals run great risks by growing old: radical expulsion from the Country of Love."[11] For the fair sex, the love market crashes at the midpoint of life, opposing older women to the younger ones, who push them off the stage. Save in rare exceptions, there is no second or third chance. The conjunction of a "boyfriend with gray temples" and a nymphet is accepted as a social fact, but the inverse is not. Whence the rage of wives whose husbands have run off with young women, with a "time delayer" (Sylvie Brunel), and who feel abandoned. The legitimate partner is reduced to the rank of confidante or a piece of furniture that has done its time, whereas the young fiancée is chiefly in danger of finding herself playing the roles of nurse and baby-sitter if the generational difference is great.[12]

People ask: what remains to women, once they are over fifty? An accepted solitude that has nothing to do with that of the tearful widows of the nineteenth century or the old maids of yesteryear but which is no less poignant. This solitude comes after a revolution in mores in the 1960s and 1970s that was supposed to guarantee equality in pleasure, whereas in fact it perpetuated an injustice. The sensual profusion promised everyone consists, for a majority of the second sex, of a crossing of a desert that is perilous or worse. They feel outdated and have to begin a trajectory all alone. The observation is implacable and apparently irrefutable, especially since women live on average five years longer than men, another inequality that should be denounced (even if it has tended to be attenuated since women have entered the job market in great numbers, smoke, drink and undergo an equivalent stress). They hang on longer, but alone and free, whereas men seem to be in a hurry to find a partner, even after becoming widowers.[13]

However, it is possible that the situation is changing, beginning with the current president of France, who is married to a woman twenty-four years his junior. It is likely that Emmanuel Macron's most important innovation in the mental landscape of his period is his matrimonial position. In matters of mores, it is the elite that sets the tone. But literature and film offer more and more examples of mature women who pair up with young men, at the risk, like their male counterparts of the same age, of sometimes having their hearts broken. In matters of love, fortune or prestige are arguments that can make anybody loveable. As soon as a woman has a certain wealth, name or status, she also acquires an additional chance to be less alone. But then she runs the same risks as old suitors: misunderstanding, deception, financial blackmail, manipulation.[14] If old rascals hang out with Lolitas, it is to be expected that mature women will be accompanied by young men. The fact that the sources of this attraction are not solely sentimental, that self-interest, careerism and shadier motives are involved, changes nothing. Relations among generations are not going to be prohibited on the ground that they don't respect morals.

But what is scandalous in these ill-matched couples, whether gay or straight, is the unacceptability of a desire that ought to be ashamed to exist. Beyond a certain limit, people are asked to confine themselves to the roles of grandparents, duennas, patriarchs or chaperones. Public opinion asks shop-worn candidates to abstain, declares their appetites inappropriate, and denounces libidinal people avid to confiscate beauty, and on this level, it is true, nature and prejudice are crueller toward women. Generally speaking, people's desirability diminishes over time, as does the price of their lives, because the latter is set, by insurance companies, on the basis of their future resources up to the foreseeable time of their death.[15] A baby is worth infinitely more than a sexagenarian, and an American more than an African or Asian. I am capital that is constantly diminishing as I grow older and, starting at a certain threshold, I will be ready for the trash heap and evaluated accordingly. The life that is beginning "is worth" more than the life that is ending. This does not mean that the life that is ending is worthless, that we should cease caring for aged patients or cease transplanting organs in patients who are over sixty-five, as some Malthusians recommend in the name of ecology.[16]

Age merely adds a chapter, the last one, to the long history of rejection that has punished the liberation of love since the 1960s. Older people suffer what all love's failures suffer: the misfortune of being rejected. And the catastrophe of exclusion begins very early. For love, from adolescence on, one word is suitable: *market*. Everyone in this trade has a grade that varies with appearance, social posture, fortune. Winners are accompanied by a cortege of suitors, losers by a multitude of rejections. Losers always end in disaster; they are wallflowers from birth onward. As the singer Juliette put it: "I've never known how to do it, I don't have the knack, I've never had any luck, I drag along and know it'll never go well ... All I know is misery, I'm alone on earth ..."[17] The game of feminine and masculine graces is subject to laws that are all the more implacable because they seem to depend on simple personal taste. In reality, under the banner of free love, a series of tacit prohibitions is deployed but never formulated as such.

Rejection is terrible because it cannot be imputed to the wickedness of the state or a social class, but only to ourselves. Sex, which in the West is in principle available to everyone, is in fact denied to many people: the declared freedom is above all the summons issued to the obscure and the ugly to resign themselves to solitude and unhappiness. Our society, by exalting everywhere and always the radiant power of pleasure, penalizes even more those who are denied it – the solitary, the old, all those refused the right to joy and a seat at the great banquet of erotic bliss. The frustration is all the greater because hedonism has been imposed as the sole norm. Erotic deregulation, inaugurated in the second half of the twentieth century, has been cruel to the weakest and to women, who have lost the most. Sometimes the excluded want to get back into the game and revolt against the discriminations of which they are the target, first and foremost "ageism." A fine symptom of the fear of growing old, among men as well as among women, is analyzing the physical defects of those close to us, in the hope that we will escape the disgraces that we have noted in them. We relentlessly examine each other to determine where we ourselves stand.

What is the taboo to be overcome when one has passed the age of fifty? Not the offense to modesty but *the ridiculous*. What, you're still at that point? That is, in the bundle of drives and appetites that constitutes the human psyche. We hesitate between bursting into laughter and being indignant. The disgusting old man is repugnant in the way the lustful grandmother is; for them, sex has become an incongruity that it would be better to wipe out entirely. However, *believing that we are now at last freed from the disorders of passion is complete nonsense: we love at sixty the way we do at twenty*; we don't change, it is others who see us differently. In the spring of 2019, the singer Madonna posted on Instagram a photo of herself with her breasts bared, and she had just turned sixty. Her fans applauded, while other people had mixed reactions.

Shameless exhibitionism, some said; a negation of decency typical of our time, others claimed. One French internet user exclaimed: "My grandmother would never have done that!" But isn't it progress that grandmothers dare to display themselves and are no longer ashamed of their bodies?

Old age embodies a twofold utopia: negatively, it is seen as death's antechamber; positively, it stands for the improbable place where we would finally be delivered from the libido, from our internal disorder. Beyond a certain limit, the calm of the senses would descend on us the way darkness falls on the countryside at dusk. Faded girls, pot-bellied Apollos, balding sugar daddies, weary playboys, and ex-belles from the beginning of the century would be compensated for their wilting by a belated detachment. At that age, we would finally realize the dream of all humanity stressed by Freud: the elimination of sexuality,[18] the aspiration to a miraculous state before the division between men and women. Because we secretly aspire to abstinence, we project it on these marked faces, these white heads that have entered the Eden of serenity. Like them, we want to bid farewell to our emotions and then to feel the passion of mastering all passions – "what pleasure is greater than disgust with pleasure?" asked Tertullian. Seneca had already demanded that we hasten to have done with carnal pleasures: "Sensual pleasure is a fragile thing that passes quickly, and is subject to disgust; the more avidly we exhaust it, the sooner it degenerates into suffering that is infallibly followed by repentance or shame."[19] Sex as we practice it today will no longer exist in sixty years, the science-fiction author Arthur C. Clarke assured us in 1993.[20] It is comforting to know that the pleasures that fatigue obliges us to forego will be dispelled once we are dead. "Old men," La Rochefoucauld already observed, "like to give good advice, since they can no longer set bad examples." Old people concentrate on themselves all the clichés formerly attributed to the noble savage: they become the virtuous negative of our errors.

The yoke of concupiscence

According to Plato (*Republic* 329b), Sophocles, having attained the age of eighty, congratulated himself on being freed from the cruel yoke of concupiscence, a "wild, hot-tempered master." That was, he said, an experience analogous to that of a people that overthrows its tyrant or to that of a slave emancipated from his owner. Cicero, citing Sophocles, says that he himself is only too happy to have escaped the power of Venus, "a harsh and unreasonable master,"[21] and confesses that he prefers abstinence to the detriment of the throes of passion. According to him, the wise man should live in the calm of the senses and be free from the thirst for honors. But Cicero himself, while offering his good advice, was carrying on a love affair with the young Publilia, who was then fourteen years old and whom he ended up marrying.[22] It will be objected that eighty is a fine age at which to resolve to be chaste, and that Victor Hugo and Picasso had, past that age, more or less furtive affairs and publicly displayed their vitality. But the Princess Palatine, a notorious seventeenth-century gossip, having been asked when desire disappeared for a woman, replied: "How should I know? I'm only eighty." Beyond the witty retort, there is perhaps a truth on which it is worth reflecting. Artists, women writers, Colette with Maurice Goudeket twenty-three years her junior, Marguerite Duras with Yann Andréa, thirty-eight years her junior (he served as the executor of her will and never got over this companionship), and Dominique Rolin with

Philippe Sollers all experienced until very late in life the beauties of attachment, of passion and of jealousy, but they were less exceptions than forerunners.

For many people, the libido, far from being a miracle, is a terrible problem that contradicts the modern dream of the uncommitted man who is his own master. To desire is still to suffer, Buddhism would say, because it is to aspire to what one does not have. Without going so far as the monk Origen, a third-century gnostic who castrated himself to reach heaven as soon as possible, it is possible to choose to extinguish, in early youth, all desire in ourselves. And to be inspired by the "renunciation of the flesh" (Peter Brown) practiced by the first Christians to prepare themselves for salvation. According to St Ambrose (c. 340–397), sex, the fact of being born male or female, constituted a fatal scar that separated us from Christ in His glory – that is, from perfection (and the gender theory borrowed from the United States is merely a contemporary rewriting of the hatred of the body and sexuality that was at the origin of our culture). Only continence could abolish the boundary between the fallen creature and his Creator.

Older people, whether men or women, are said to have entered *the fascinating era of subtraction*. In them, time is supposed to have overcome the disorder of the senses. The best remedy for erotic license therefore resides in the happy sphere of advanced age. To be sure, many couples grow old without being disturbed by the flesh; they love each other enough and have no need to prove their passion. Many, but not all: desire does not miraculously disappear after sixty, and healthy people in their seventies or eighties continue to feel an imperious need for sex. Not everyone accepts being relieved of this burden, and some wish to persist in enjoying carnal pleasure as long as possible. There are at least two kinds of happiness: a happiness of calming and a happiness of intensity. The former is the privation of pain, the latter a quest for strong satisfactions. These two kinds of happiness can alternate in the same person, depending on the day or the period. In one case, the feeling of well-being comes from the lessening of tensions. In the other, it reflects the search for beautiful sensations. The former is in general associated with maturity, the latter with the impetuosity of youth. But "that accidental repentance that age brings" (Montaigne) sometimes strikes in adolescence, whereas adolescence returns, like a kind of remorse or miracle, in a late period. Like certain schools in Antiquity, we can wish to abolish desire, to steal the soul away from the tumult of Eros. Or, inversely, we can celebrate our drives, those powerful forces that attach us to the earth and the charms of the world.

At every age we have a choice between a fertile torment and a bland well-being. That is the difficulty: great maturity is criss-crossed by appetites without having the authorization to manifest them. The body is supposed to settle down in the measure that it loses the sap of youth. But we don't know everything that a body is capable of (Spinoza), what degree of excess it can reach. There are more resources in us than we think. That is why some people – like Sartre, according to Michel Contat – practice the "full employment of their bodies" right up to the end, convinced of their unlimited potential.

HEROES SUPERIOR TO US

To live is always to admire what transcends us, to take the unique beings, male or female, as models whose conduct gives us strength and hope. That is why we often prefer biographies to fictions: we are fascinated especially by the trajectories of people who have fallen, bitten the dust and gotten up again. These twists and turns in the life of an exceptional individual give meaning and shape to our own. In his eulogy of old age, Cicero was right: exceptional persons are also located in the rarefied spaces of age where a careless observer sees only weakness and weariness. We decipher them passionately to find out where we will be at this crucial moment. The example of a human being is worth all the principles of philosophy. There are two ways of conceiving maturity: as a cliff that casts us into desolation or as a softly sloping meadow that slowly leads toward the end. Even a gradual decline has many ups and downs. The respect that certain individuals inspire goes beyond the simple performance of longevity (Immanuel Kant). Admiration for these great figures – think Simone Veil, Claude Lévi-Strauss, Marguerite Yourcenar – is inseparable from their ability to cope with adversity. They remain models not because of their age but despite it, because their lives are radiant with originality and surprises. It is in the creative domain that our astonishment is greatest. Consider octogenarian film directors such as Clint Eastwood, Woody Allen and Roman Polanski, who continue to work unceasingly, giving the lie to all the clichés; consider Edgar Morin, who continues to publish at the age of ninety-eight, or the Portuguese director Manoel de Oliveira, who was still making films when he was over a hundred; consider again the prodigious pianist Martha Argerich, eighty, or the sculptor Louise Bourgeois (1911–2010), who worked up to the last. By themselves, these figures render obsolete countless treatises and make ageing seem almost desirable. Emissaries of humanity on these far-off continents, they tell us that, over there, life is not only not diminished but still possible and even unpredictable. They are the avant-garde on the path of life, drawing behind them the frightened flock of the recalcitrant.

Indecent requests

If becoming an adult means learning to rank one's desires, living past that age paradoxically means cultivating and even multiplying them. Descartes demanded that we overcome our desires rather than the world order. But defeated desire wants to return surreptitiously and triumph, even if only for a brief moment, over the world order. With this nuance: past a certain threshold, it has to advance wearing a mask and enveloped in tactfulness. Then we have to court other people's consent, and even *faire sa cour*, to use a term from the Ancien Régime. This old-fashioned discipline, which is violently rejected by neo-feminists and is called galanterie, has never been more important, for men as well as for women. A graybeard and a cougar have to show elegance in their proposals and not copy adolescents' impetuousness. Seniors are love's marranos, forced to dissimulate to be accepted. At this altitude, carnal appetite has to remain discreet, on pain of sinking into bawdy senility. One of old age's flaws is too often a lack of manners, the disappearance of censorship: completely unknown people approach you, sit down at your table as if you were old friends and, on the pretext of vague relations or a simple coincidence of birthdates, settle in. You belong to them solely because you ran into them one day on a sidewalk.

How is that possible, we wonder sometimes when we see certain mismatched couples: ravishing young creatures associated with repulsive patriarchs, Dionysian bodies alongside gnarled fossils. Beauty and the Beast, the comely and the misshapen. Our aesthetic sense rebels, accompanied by a vague jealousy. Too many people don't see themselves getting old and imagine that they are, after fifty, as attractive as a twenty-year-old. Nothing is beautiful enough for them; they wink encouragingly, eager to bewitch the objects of their desire! But the hypnotizer is mistaken. The *old coquette* believes she is irresistible and simpers, certain that she will enchant her prey. The *old Lothario* persists, conducts an assiduous campaign, sure that he will soon overcome his belle's resistance. Both are the puppets of their conceit, converting rejections into proofs of seduction. "If I'd wished, he or she would have fallen for me like a ripe fruit." That's how reputations are preserved and consolations strengthened. The same narcissism that used to serve them now destroys them. In this domain, men, let's admit it, are the most pathetic: little old men with ponytails flanked by girls who could be their daughters or even their granddaughters, too concerned with looking eternally young in the eyes of their pals. Old gaffers hovering around young women with their flattering smiles, their exaggerated politeness, their pompous compliments. They are masters of the superlative. They are allowed to carry on, as a testimony to earlier mores, because *it goes nowhere*. From a certain point on, the peacock's dance is above all a capon's contortion. Hormones at half-mast, herbal teas in abundance ... and reducing the tea doesn't awaken the hormones.

At a certain age, there is also a great temptation to yield to slovenliness. Untidy baby-boomers, both men and women, imagine that they are still dashing when they are only unkempt. To grow old is also to capitulate, and capitulation begins with sagging, the body left to itself like a fallow field. Passing time often transforms the human being into a digestive tube that ingests and drinks, for lack of something better. What else is there, apart from addiction to filling out? Michel Tournier remarked that there are two ways of ageing: getting fat and getting skinny. Some people swell up, developing puffy faces and blotchy skin striated with creases. Others dry out, reduce their anatomy to a stick, with fleshless faces, all skin and bone. Rotundity conceals the wrinkles; thinness accentuates them "like knife-blows," reveals the skeleton beneath the tunic of the epidermis. Whether one ages in the comfort of a chubby body or the restriction of an emaciated one, whether one is a scrawny, mumbling old man or a former fat man who has melted away, it is never easy to accept, at every stage, what one has become. And since the generation of the 1970s reintroduced the requirement of naturalness in opposition to the artificiality of manners, many of its members continue, after sixty years, to maintain the same look, with baggy clothes, scruffy tee-shirts, worn-out jeans, miniskirts or clingy shorts. They absolutely want to retain the uniform of their thirties, to pretend they haven't changed. Carelessness allows them to show their pride and reject being told how they should look, the dictatorship of appearances. They had put all their ardor into remaining young; now they're old and everyone knows it, except them.

Former Don Juans believe they're as vigorous as stallions, and man-eaters claim to have uterine passions worthy of courtesans. But Don Juan has shrunk, and Messalina is tired. The tragedy of the accumulating years is that we don't see ourselves changing until strangers straighten us out. Sartre said poetically that he gave women beautiful objects to make them forget his ugliness. Similarly, many people think they are impudent when they are only bawdy, rattling on and on. "Am I not still Casanova today as I used to be? And, if I am, why shouldn't the odious law to which other people are subject, and which is called getting old, be abolished in my case?,"[23] asks Arthur Schnitzler's sixty-year-old character. So speaks all-powerful egoism. It's hard to know whether to laugh or weep.

THE BRAGGART AND THE COMPLAINER

There are two opposed, very characteristic types of human beings. Braggarts, whether men or women, claim to be in perfect health, to enjoy a dazzling success, to have convincing erections or staggering orgasms, and not to feel the weight of time. They talk on and on, look with pity on people of their age, make fun of their jeremiads. They are regularly found in the emergency room, afflicted with various complaints that weaken them. They recover, say they never felt better, then relapse. There is a kind of heroism in their boastfulness; if one day they are swept away, struck by a heart attack or carried off by cancer, they will succumb with dignity, refusing to bow down before destiny. Their counterparts are the complainers: every day finds them falling victim to a new affliction and sends them running off to see the doctor. Since they turned twenty, they've been convinced that they will die the following week, and that's been going on for the past forty years. They are among those perpetual invalids who survive longer than the healthy. They hurt all over, want us to pity their fate, but refuse to allow others to talk about their own little troubles. Your suffering is insignificant compared with theirs. Even your cancer is small alongside their rheumatism, your pericarditis far from being as serious as their pulmonary embolism. They will bury us all and, once their friends are dead, will no longer have anyone to whom they can confide their little pains.

6

Eros and Agape in the Shadow of Thanatos

"Whether you believe it or not, Mademoiselle Lola has always
had a weakness for middle-aged gentlemen. And not only
because of that ..." She rubbed her thumb and index finger
against one another.
"... But because she has a good heart. That's what older
gentlemen need, more than others, to be treated kindly."

HEINRICH MANN[1]

It is an odd experience to see again Mike Nichols's cult
film *The Graduate*, which came out in 1967. At the age
of twenty, we sympathized unreservedly with Benjamin
(played by Dustin Hoffmann), a distressed young man who
is seduced by an older married woman, Mrs Robinson
(played by Anne Bancroft, who was thirty-six at the time
the film was made). Now, we are intrigued by the seduc-
tress; she is doubly guilty, both of deceiving her husband
and of desiring outside her age group. But she doesn't
care that she might be wrecking her family; and, when
Benjamin becomes engaged to marry her daughter, she

continues to sleep with him, so that the shadow of incest now hovers over the action. The richness of this film, which is full of subtleties, is that it can be considered from the angle of each character: it defends simultaneously the difficulty of growing up, the rights of youthful love and the rights of mature desire with regard to conventional desire. And when at the end the young people escape on a bus, their smiling faces suddenly freeze: true matrimonial life is coming into view, rich with joys but also with dangerous burdens.

Just as audacious and disturbing is the film *Harold and Maude*, which came out in 1971. It is the story of an unemployed post-adolescent Californian who is fascinated by suicide, and to whom his mother presents, to distract him, a series of potential mates that he discourages by cutting his hand in front of them or by disembowelling himself with a trick butcher knife. He falls in love with the sparkling Maude, a deliciously zany eighty-year-old lady who is a former concentration camp prisoner. She is obsessed by burials and auto thefts and ends up poisoning herself.[2] To these, we must add *Summer of '42*,[3] a deeply moving film about a fifteen-year-old adolescent who is spending his vacation on the island of Nantucket in the middle of World War II. Eager to lose his virginity, at any cost, he falls in love with a woman of thirty whose husband has gone to war, and who dies in Europe. She gives herself to him for one night and then disappears forever.

The seducer, the eccentric octogenarian, the initiator: these three films testify, each in its own way, to a genuine understanding of the meanders of desire between young men and mature women.

Devotees of the twilight

Although long-term couples remain in the majority and experience, at the cost of numerous crises, an uninterrupted companionship, the remarriage of widowers and widows takes place under the sign of a value that is the great conquest of the age: indulgence. It is a cohabitation, temperate or passionate, marked by the tolerance of each other's imperfections. The physical expectations are smaller because the spiritual expectations are greater. Complicity and tenderness are given priority over vanity.

In other words, one of the solutions for the injustices of desire, apart from strengthening women's economic and political power, is to change the public's view regarding the marks of time. It is not necessarily found in a certain literature – which is a little plaintive – but rather on the internet, on sites where a new feminine sexuality is deployed with a tranquil modesty, in the anonymity of tips and networks. Since everything is permissible and users are masked by a pseudonym, the least commendable longings can be revealed without shame to partners of every age group, who are eager for sensations. People look for a kindred soul as much as for ephemeral sexual encounters. Social networks accelerate mentalities on this level: women and men offer themselves without embarrassment in sort of ultimate libertinage. They know how to make themselves attractive despite their sagging flesh, how to convert the undesirable into the attractive.[4]

In a given population, there will always be a certain percentage of men and women who are attracted by older people. Let us call this penchant *the ambiguous nobility of ruins: the memory of past splendor plus the sweetness of decline.* In it, the eternal has the charm of the precarious, that of friable skins, elegant lacerations, forms sculpted by time. Repulsion, with regard to aesthetic criteria, can be inverted into attraction (Sade's whole work testifies to this, reflecting the metamorphosis of disgust into pleasure and even into delight). In every society there exist "devotees of the twilight" who like the company of mature persons to reassure themselves, to compare themselves, to console themselves, to broaden their minds, to get drunk on their expertise, to enjoy the charms of an erudite or brilliant conversation.[5] There is beauty in the ruins, and it is possible that age does not destroy a face so much as it consecrates it. All parts of the body do not age in the same way: here are youthful smiles on weary faces, immemorial looks on childlike faces. Some babies look like old men with pacifiers, and some old men display a toddler's candor.

We must multiply amorous women with gray hair.

The tragedy of the last love

What are people looking for in these mismatched couples? To shift the burden of their age onto other people who give them their freshness in return, to exchange experience for immaturity. "It was in my nature and the circumstances of my youth to fall in love with a woman sufficiently haloed with prestige that I would lay at her feet the wreath of my too-long-withheld favors, and there was a very good chance that this woman would be older than I," wrote Maurice Goudeket, the last husband of Colette, whom he met in April 1925, when she was fifty-two and he was thirty-six. They married in 1935, and she died in 1954 (five years later he married Sanda Dancovici, with whom he had a child, and he died in 1977). Let us further consider the passionate relationship of "sexualized angels" between the writers Philippe Sollers and Dominique Rolin, who was twenty-three years older than he. An incompletely resolved Oedipus complex, the quest for an absent father or a missing mother, the need for an initiator or a Pygmalion? Maybe. So what? Do we have to show a certificate of analytical purity to be admitted to the banquet of love?

It is a matter not only of rejuvenating or renewing the objects of desire but of understanding that *desire alone is a factor that rejuvenates the heart and soul*, that it constantly gives birth to us. "Old age? You were lying: a route of embers, not of ashes," wrote Saint-John Perse. In his book *Le Nouveau Monde industriel et sociétaire*, the utopian thinker Charles Fourier (1772–1837) imagines the love affair of Urgèle, an eighty-year-old "hyperfairy" versed in horticulture, who loves Valère, twenty. Valère is united with her by a pure bond of gratitude, friendship and ambition, because she has initiated him, along with others, into the floral art. "Youth is intrepid in love when it has sufficient stimulants." It's a question of overcoming the natural antipathies between striplings and old people and of promoting sympathy and harmony where prejudices exclude them. Young people compete in "amorous devotion" to their elders, who take delight in listening to their confidences and in caressing their charms.

Experiencing strong emotions – in the broadest sense of the term – luck, pleasure, good fortune, and enjoying all the kindnesses of the world is not reserved for people under fifty. Even if one has lived a full life, there remains much to do before bringing down the curtain. And in particular this: to rediscover routine as a miracle. What youth, completely absorbed in squandering its inexhaustible strength, accomplishes automatically, maturity accomplishes with greater difficulty.[6] In any case, let us rejoice that the concern about flagging virility among men and a declining sex drive among women is being attenuated by medical science, which combats erectile dysfunction in the former and the end of sexual appetite in the latter. Women's complaints about amorous loneliness correspond to the organic apocalypse of men describing with desperation the loss of their libido[7] and their prostate problems. There is no miraculous medical solution, of course, but this much is certain: with time, everything that was routine, in the erotic domain, becomes rarer, and therefore more precious. "Love is of no importance," said Alfred Jarry, "because it can be made indefinitely." That is no longer true beyond a certain age, when each embrace becomes once again a marvel. Reason commands us to withdraw from the world, but desire commands us to plunge one last time into the flames of pleasure and love.

But this sometimes rejuvenated heart is also and often a bruised heart. Experiencing great joys to the end means increasing the risk of great suffering. Whence the tragedy of the last love, when the adored person is closed to you like a slamming door and puts an end to your hopes: there will be no one else, there will be no afterward. Madly in love with Jeanne Loviton, known as Jean Voilier, an editor who turned the heads of many celebrities during the interwar period, Paul Valéry (1871–1945) wrote to her after she had left him: "I believed you were between me and death; now I realize that I was between you and life." What's so terrible about the last love is that it deprives us of even the sorrows of the first one. At the age of twenty, being abandoned or betrayed leaves you devastated, on the edge of suicide. The last love longs even for that devastation, the irrepressible tears, the absolute annihilation. In contrast, it is a silent collapse. And the ditched old lover or mistress is not even touching in the eyes of others, just grotesque, discordant like an out-of-tune piano. They simply got what they deserved! What an idea to get mixed up with someone younger and to harbor hopes? Really, did they realize how they looked?

You will no longer suffer, no longer wait, heart pounding, for your beloved to call or to return, no longer endure the contempt, the hurtful words, the cruelty that were still sweet to you because they were inflicted by your beloved. You even went so far as to cherish the nastiness, the betrayals, debasing yourself abjectly for the simple pleasure of being still connected with her. The person you adored the most in the world has sent you packing and gone off to see what's available elsewhere. She (or he) was everything for you, but for her you were no more than a stage, a stopgap. She was practicing sentimental tourism, making an excursion into the country of senility; you were risking your life. She lent you youth, then took it back. The scratch marks of time become once again what they ceased to be in the brief moment of crystallization: marks of banishment. If every person met is a possible world that unfolds, the last love signals the end of all possible worlds. The person who has left takes on the face of the irremediable. You naïvely think you are playing a trick on destiny, benefiting from additional thrills. Age has caught up with you; you won't escape the common fate. You will no longer experience those vertiginous alternations between extreme lust and extreme modesty. Farewell to everything that made life valuable, farewell to waiting, smiling, tears, spasms, incandescence and even despair. The embers have become ashes.

The chaste, the tender and the voluptuous

The crisis of marriage for love arose, as we know, from the lengthening of life as much as from the inconstancy of the human heart. In the seventeenth or eighteenth century, swearing fidelity at the age of twenty did not have the same meaning when death might well strike you between twenty-five and thirty, whereas making the same oath in 2019 may signify sixty years of life together. Beyond the always sensitive question of adultery, we can glimpse the hope of remarriage made easier by the law: in democratic countries, divorce has become a simple and always expensive formality (it is now possible to get divorced online). After fifty-five or sixty, children are generally raised, retirement is being planned, and spouses see new horizons opening up before them. Setting out on another idyll tempts the reason of more than one person. People separate as often at the age of sixty as they do at thirty, and the majority of those who leave are women.

No matter what one goes through then, steamy encounters or modest caresses, what counts no longer resides in performance but in the ardent complicity, the willing abandon. On these subjects, modesty and discretion must be left up to the individuals involved. Myth or reality, some statisticians claim that women who are great lovers live longer. Let us welcome this good news, even if, in this domain, prudence is recommended.[8] "I'm seventy-four," Jane Fonda said early in the twenty-first century, "and I've never had such a fulfilling sex life." Let's be happy for her and take her at her word. One thing is certain: love, at any age, awakens us, justifies our existence. I become the creator of the other by cherishing her as she re-creates me in turn. "Saying 'I love you' to someone is to say: you will not die" – an admirable sentence by Gabriel Marcel. To love is also to be glad that the other exists and to rejoice in still being alive to tell her so every day. Two is never too many to enjoy the sweetness of life, to prevent the succession of days from being gratuitous, to transfigure the perpetual stammering of everyday life. What did you do today? Hardly anything, but this little something is not the same when I can discuss it with you as it is when I have to ruminate on it in solitude. At every moment we need a kindly ear to which we can confide our worries, our unhappiness, and at every moment we are needed to listen to the other to console and counsel her.

Shared predilections, attention to small events, bond two persons better than resounding declarations. The fragility of human affairs is never so perceptible and moving as it is in those moments. A close couple is an uninterrupted conversation, a common appetite for reading, travel, inexhaustible encounters. It's up to each partner to preserve his own *sanctuary*, what is most dear to him – family, children, loves without which he would waste away. The essential point is to remain in a state of permanent fever, even when it is punctuated by doubt or melancholy. So long as eyes can covet, hands caress and lips kiss, a brand-new heart beats in our breast, even at eighty, and infuses an *élan vital* in us.

In our youth, we can choose asceticism rather than pleasures and construct ourselves against our own concupiscence. There comes a time when it is the absence of flame that predominates, when the fear is no longer desiring too much but no longer desiring at all. The rigidification of the body foretells that of the heart. The quest, specific to Stoicism, for an imperturbable soul, sealed off from emotions, the will to become a being who "neither hopes nor fears" (Seneca) and is self-sufficient with what he has, constitutes, alas, not the *summum* of self-mastery but a simple, flat, sinister description of the end of life. The Ancients, and the classical age of the seventeenth century, feared the ravages of the passions that led people into disorder and indignity, whereas we fear, more than anything, the bankruptcy of the senses, estrangement from desire.

That's the problem with self-control: over time, it ends up succeeding so well that there's nothing more to control and everything to awaken. Desire used to be described as a torrent that sweeps away proprieties as it passes and against which dikes and dams must be erected. Soon enough, alas, it shrinks to a rivulet, as volatile as it is inconstant. Who wouldn't be prepared to do anything to know once again the marvel of a budding inclination, or even a love affair for life? A person who has lived is one who has encountered eternity in time, through love and friendship, and has known the feeling of existing in close proximity to Being. The real tragedy is one day to stop loving and desiring, to dry up the twofold spring that attaches us to the world and to others. The opposite of sexuality is not abstinence, it is being tired of living. As the great St Augustine said: "Lord, make me chaste, but not yet." Life says yes to life, being is better than nothingness, desire is preferable to apathy. When Eros and Agape fall silent, Thanatos has already won.

THE FAREWELL OF THE OLD SPOUSES

They pass close to us, often unnoticed, the braver of the two supporting the healthier, as the blind man supports the paralytic; every step is an effort, they excuse themselves for existing, make themselves as small as they can, persist. They seem so fragile, so shaky, that we fear they will break down at any moment. They have bad eyesight, can hardly hear, tremble a little. They wait patiently in railway stations, doctors' waiting rooms and government offices, keeping an eye on their watches or the clocks, always on the alert, lost in a world that ignores them, pushes them aside. The slightest problem or technical complication terrifies them. Running their errands, buying bread and milk, carrying the grocery sack, typing in a code, getting money from a cash dispenser, is a torture for them. Every excursion, every walk, includes a risk. Petty criminals try to rob them, grab their property and panic them by raising their voices. A simple trip by bus or the underground is a trial. A swerve, a misstep, and they go crashing down. Going up or down a stairway is an ordeal: they have to stop on every step to catch their breath. Mercy for the most vulnerable!

What will happen to them if one of them dies? They are two weaknesses aiding each other, but together they compose only a weakness squared. She is in him as he is in her. Mingled with each other like the roots of a tree, they form one and the same person endowed with two faces and two names. So the pain of one becomes the pain of the other. "I'm the one who suffers when my wife's legs hurt," said the Spanish philosopher Miguel de Unamuno magnificently. It also happens that a serious illness, striking one of them, convinces the other to follow him, and that they decide to die together. In September 2007, that was the case of the writer André Gorz and his wife, who had an incurable disease: "You have just turned eighty-two," he wrote in a book dedicated to her. "You have shrunk by 6 centimeters, you weigh only 45 kilos, and you are still beautiful, gracious, desirable. We have been living together for fifty-eight years and I love you more than ever."[9] For such people, it is inconceivable to remain on earth after the death of the beloved. Before them, other couples, such as the former socialist senator Roger Quilliot and his wife, had decided to die at the same moment, finding gaiety and serenity once again before the curtain went down. (Unfortunately for her, the pills they swallowed did not kill Claire Quilliot. She finally succeeded in committing suicide in 2005, at the age of seventy-nine, by jumping into a lake in Puy-de-Dôme after swallowing drugs, like her favorite author, Virginia Woolf, whom she admired.) Why allow dreadful nature to dictate what you do, and deprive you of the only person who counts, when you can make the journey together? People kill themselves to ward off not the fear of death but, rather, the living death that is loneliness without the essential person. In addition to the romanticism of youth, there is also sometimes the sublime romanticism of an old married couple. Suicide, John Donne wrote, bears its own absolution because, unlike sin, it can be committed only once.

PART IV

Fulfill Oneself or Forget Oneself?

CHAPTER 7

No More, Too Late, Still!

On a recent drive through rural Ohio, I saw signs put
up by a local real estate dealer. Instead of the customary
"Sold," these read: "Sorry, too late." Exactly so. If there
are tombstones for hope, this is their epitaph.

GEORGE STEINER[1]

The luck of having talent does not suffice; you also have to
have the talent of being lucky.

HECTOR BERLIOZ

The photographer Brassaï tells us that Marcel Proust,
when he was a young man, became infatuated with a
Genevan boy, Edgar Aubert, but did not dare declare his
love.[2] On the back of the photograph that the boy gave
Proust was inscribed the following dedication, in English,
taken from a sonnet by the pre-Raphaelite painter Dante
Gabriel Rossetti: "Look at my face; my name is might have
been, I am also called No More, Too Late, Farewell."

Lost opportunities

A gesture taken back, an unspoken word, a hand not offered, and we miss a person, an affair that might have ravaged us. We imagine them being all the more splendid because they did not take place. We haven't taken advantage of the opportunity; we should have improvised, on the spot, immediately, shown initiative. These are moments when, out of fear, shock or timidity, our fate does not change. We lacked presence of mind. And if others act, in our place, show themselves audacious, we resent them. How can we forgive ourselves for being pusillanimous? The next time, for sure, we'll be up to it, we'll dazzle the person desired with a stupefying proposition.

We often accord these failed godsends excessive credit. We are like Baudelaire with regard to a woman who is walking in front of him, "Agile and noble, with her leg like a statue's": "Oh I would have loved you, oh you who knew it!" One may doubt this conditional mood: we become all the more infatuated with strangers because in their case we will be spared the most redoubtable test: everyday life, which dissolves everything. With time, a person who initially enchants me may become a harridan I long to be rid of. How can I know whether this person chanced upon will turn out to be just another illusion? The encounter is heart-rending only because it remains unfinished. Our regrets, especially late in life, pass through our memory like phantom pains felt in an amputated limb. Their motor is the past conditional: I should have! All that remains is to feel sorry for oneself for failing to act. What might have happened becomes more important than what actually occurred; the virtual eats away the real and devalues it. The hope that chance, that intermittent god, will provide us *ex abrupto* with a great destiny is typical of the person nostalgic for lost opportunities. The shroud of his vanished desires worries him more than his realized ambitions. A single question torments him: how can the accidental be transformed into a benediction, the aleatory into an enchantment?

Too late, too soon. Some people's lives remain completely devoted to what has not been realized – what might have been and now will never be. All through their lives, they content themselves with living in the past conditional or the future perfect, and everyone could write the history of his destinies avoided, which accompany him like so many ghosts conjured up when he is depressed. Then we dwell on the sad catalogue of our aborted projects. If you had gotten a higher score on the doctoral examination, if I had continued my studies, if I had gone to live in the East, if I had married this person or that! I deserved better, my fate is not the one I should have! Thus there are people, both men and women, who want to live many other possible lives for lack of living at least one of them, their own. To them, everything seems preferable to the tasteless brew of their condition. They were born at the wrong time; their century, their partner, their school, their friends are all wrong. They are briefly infatuated with everyone they meet or pass by, like so many existential crutches, envying them because they don't consider their own condition.

Here we could draw up a typology of punctuality in both ordinary life and history: the paranoiac comes ahead of time, a little defiantly, to be sure that he is expected and, if possible, to get there before the others, even if only by a minute or two. In that regard, there is nothing worse than an alarm clock that rings ahead of time and tortures you with its stridency when you're trying to grab a few more minutes' sleep, or a tiresome person who slips in a few minutes before your appointment and presents himself, all proud of his annoying exactitude. The narcissist is late on principle: he likes to make himself desired at the risk of exasperating those around him; he defers his engagements, wants to test the attachment devoted to him, especially in that crucial situation where every minute counts, the lover's rendezvous. He temporizes, capriciously indecisive. He has elevated procrastination to the level of an ethics. Those are two ways of resisting the despotism of the clock, by extreme meticulousness and by casualness. Only the ordinary neurotic worships rigor and arrives on time, stupidly on time, astonished that people are astonished, not even needing to glance at his watch.

Punctuality is a recent invention in Europe. It appeared in the sixteenth century, in Geneva, the homeland of Calvinism, along with the improvement of watches and other instruments for measuring time. There is also an anthropology and a geography of time: everywhere, and especially in the countries of Southern Europe, an elasticity of schedules that allows a good quarter of an hour's delay. Being punctual then amounts almost to a lack of *savoir-vivre* or a cultural misunderstanding. It is said that, at the end of the nineteenth century, the Gare d'Orsay delayed train departures by a few minutes to give latecomers a chance – a thoughtful practice. If young people are often annoyed by schedules, they have lots of time ahead of them, and we see retirees who continue to get up at dawn, as if to go to the office, and then wander around looking for something to do, impatiently awaiting mealtime, which will give them a reason for being. The yoke of work continues to weigh on them, but without the content that was its cause. To live under the tyranny of dials, like the White Rabbit in *Alice in Wonderland*, who is constantly looking at his pocket watch instead of at nature and others, is to doom oneself to being "late, always late," because the second hand is constantly moving and we get out of breath trying to keep up with it. The exact time is never the exact time; it slips through our fingers every second.

What about historical punctuality? Must we be in the avant-garde of our period, coincide with it, or deliberately trail behind it? Or should we combine all three positions? Sometimes it's not a bad thing to be behind one's century or one's generation: being the youngest child in a large family, the ex-chancellor of Germany Helmut Kohl spoke of "the favor of a late birth,"[3] taking his examinations after everyone else, marrying and having children long after the official age – in short, living after others and claiming the fine title of an anachronic. That grants you a long range of new years, a fine future already lived by most people but which you will take elsewhere simply because you came last. Sometimes you have to miss an appointment with history in order to be ahead of it. That is the *survivor's privilege*: thus the French philosopher Alain Badiou, the last-born of the structuralist generation, attained a certain fame only at the age of seventy, long after the death of the great figures of that period, Barthes, Foucault, Deleuze, Lyotard, Derrida, Bourdieu. Hence he can recapitulate them, judge them, give them last rites. The survivor takes charge of the dead and appears to be their synthesis, when in fact he is only a remote offshoot.

Each life is erected on the rejection or exclusion of other projects. Or, rather, it benefits from a crime: that of killing virtualities that were consequently not able to blossom. The event is fatal and eliminates those that could have been substituted for it. The temptation is great, later on, to want to recuperate these abandoned possibilities, to give them new energy and allow them to develop. Even if we know that there are new potential departures, that the chips are never down, it remains that what has happened compromises what could have happened. Whether we want to be or not, we are still prisoners of our acts. And, for those who don't receive the favor of a second, third or fourth chance, the time of the shortage of possibilities begins there. Hands cease to reach out, days remain poor in adventures, the path no longer twists: it is all laid out, hopelessly flat. That is how certain public figures disappear; suddenly, we hear nothing more about them and their names resound only on the day of their death, when everyone has already forgotten them. Time reduces uncertainty even if, at certain privileged moments, there seems to be in us more wealth than we will ever be able to know. Then we are tormented by the dream of escaping from this self that weighs on us, from this past heavy as a cannon ball, and go in search of the saving episode from which "everyone has the right to expect the revelation of the meaning of his life" (André Breton).

THE FAMILY OF OUR DECEASED

Starting in our fifties, we are astonished to still be vigorous, whereas so many others have already bowed out. Funerals become as frequent as marriages or baptisms. We live with our contemporaries as much as with our dead, whom we summon at will, as we will someday be summoned. We skim through the obituary columns with mixed feelings, sometimes looking to be sure that someone hasn't listed our name by mistake. Another one: he was, after all, rather young to die. Did he suffer? What were his last words? Who decided about the funeral? Religious or secular? What piece of music did he choose? Will he be cremated or buried? In a sign of the disappearance of collective rituals, each person now reinvents his interment as he wishes.

An admirable remark by Zola regarding Gustave Flaubert, who was killed by apoplexy in 1880: "A fine

---

death, an enviable sledgehammer blow that made me wish for myself and for all those I love this annihilation, like an insect crushed under a giant finger." We can envy others for everything, even their death. In their misfortune, they were lucky. In this regard, funeral meals are a reinvigorating tradition: the living feast to keep Death away, they repel it with forkfuls of food and toasts. The army of the deceased allows us to withstand the onslaught, still valiant despite those who fall. The quiet pride taken in always being active is compensated by the fear of being the next on the list. A mission is assigned us, to make ourselves witnesses and the spokesmen for these deceased persons whom we represent on earth. They live in our hearts, in our words, in our memories. We resuscitate them by speaking of them; they are our dead, the family of our deceased, the round of shades that inhabit us and do not leave us until we breathe our last.

As the final date approaches, another obligation arises: not to make a mess of our exit and not to leave, any more than necessary, the decision to the moral or medical authorities. Biological survival is not the ultimate value: freedom and dignity are superior to it. When we have lost our autonomy and the ability to share in the world with others, when eating, breathing and sleeping have become almost torture, it is time to leave, to bow out. Elegantly, if possible. As did the great Belgian writer Hugo Claus on 19 March 2008. Afflicted by Alzheimer's disease, suffering from motor difficulties and rejecting the consequent decline, he went, dressed in his best suit, to the Middelheim Hospital in Antwerp, accompanied by his wife and a friend who was a publisher. After finishing off a bottle of champagne and smoking a cigarette, he lay down and, in a serene atmosphere, underwent anaesthesia and a lethal injection. This is authorized in Belgium if the patient has submitted a "voluntary and well-considered" request. A great lord's way of taking his leave.

The round of regrets

Too late: all the marvellous things we haven't seen, tasted, sung, enjoyed, the admirable people who made eyes at us and then turned their backs on us, annoyed by our indifference. The woman we weren't able to love, whom we left for wild dreams and whom we caused to suffer for nothing, the friend so dear to us whom we neglected and who left too soon, the overflowing maternal love that exasperated us and that we now miss. The time is past! Our best days are over! Remorse gnaws at us. If I had it to do over, if only I were twenty years younger! – says the melancholic. It is likely, alas!, that he would make the same mistakes with the same certainty of being right. We know those stories, those films, in which the characters go back to the past to avoid a catastrophe, to change a genealogy, to prevent a fatal incest. (For instance, *Back to the Future*,[4] in which a young woman in a small American town falls in love with her son, sent by mistake back to the 1950s. The son's whole effort is directed toward guiding his future mother's interest toward his future father.) We simple mortals lack the power enjoyed by dictatorial regimes to rewrite history, erase faces, retouch photos.

We are always lucid after the fact, and only then do we recognize the signs of what was to come: If only I had known! Understanding comes after the error, and, as Hegel said, "Minerva's owl [the symbol of wisdom] takes flight only at dusk." If we didn't take the plunge, that is probably because we didn't want to. Regret is as sterile as it is inevitable. The eternal alibi of defeatism: it's too late to resume studies, too late to take a long journey, too late to fall in love in again. I've done my time, says the unadventurous person. At eighty as at twenty, there is still time, boldness consisting in not succumbing to the fatality of the irreversible. But *Too late* can also be a mad, unhoped-for stroke of luck: the plane that we have missed by just a few minutes crashes an hour after taking off without leaving a single survivor. Is it luck or a monstrous coincidence? Are we going to systematically miss all our planes to escape a possible accident? At the risk, says the paranoiac, that the later plane we take is precisely the one that is going to go down in a crash ...

The same goes for *Too soon*. It leaves promises intact: they continue to shine in the future. Precociousness does not destroy possibilities, a setback is not crippling. No, not now, not right away, says the beloved to her eager suitor; that would spoil the marvellous indecision. Let's wait a little longer. I'm not ready – let me dream a moment more. Any haste would be a sacrilege. *Too soon*: that is also the tragedy of hypochondriacs. From the age of twenty on, they have been convinced that they are going to die: the slightest pimple is a tumor that is growing, a mosquito bite will degenerate into blood poisoning, a leg cramp foreshadows paralysis, a headache is a sign of a stroke. We laugh at these childish fears. But hypochondriacs are wrong only because they are right too soon. The disease they diagnose today will strike them someday. They are just ahead of schedule. What terrorizes them may happen later, when they have forgotten it. And then they will recognize with dismay that their youthful fears were justified.

All adverbs of time recount a particular tragedy or hope: in that regard, *never again* is an ambiguous expression. It can signify the violent pain of the irremediable, of love forever lost, as in Poe's *The Raven* (with its "Nevermore")[5] or, as at the end of Simone de Beauvoir's *La Force des choses*:

> Yes, the moment has come to say: Never again! It is not I who am saying good-bye to all those things I once enjoyed, it is they who are leaving me; the mountain paths disdain my feet. Never again shall I collapse, drunk with fatigue, into the smell of hay. Never again shall I slide down through the solitary morning snows. Never again a man.[6]

But this classic sorrow over the passage of time does not sum up by itself the profundity of the Nevermore. The writer Italo Svevo denounces a mendacious promise implicit in it, but it is an almost sacred promise that it is appropriate to violate only in order to save its substance. Keeping one's word would make words useless, empty them of their content. With a kind of jubilation of failure, it inverts here the terms of the promise. The hero, as we have said, has been swearing for years to smoke a last cigarette: "I even tried to give a philosophical content to the last-cigarette disease. Striking a beautiful attitude, one says: 'Never again.' But what becomes of that attitude if the promise is then kept? It's possible to strike the attitude only when you are obliged to renew the vow."[7] Because the last cigarette has more flavor when it accompanies the feeling of winning a victory over oneself and allows him to hope for an "imminent future of strength and health," the character is going to cover the walls of his room with peremptory dates for stopping smoking and bury his vice forever. The "Never again" on which Europe was based after 1945 has never prevented massacres from occurring on our soil (including those in the Yugoslav wars), as if the spectacle of the crime committed before our eyes necessarily renewed the urgency of the solemn commitment made to future generations. Thomas Jefferson said it cynically: "The tree of liberty must be refreshed from time to time with the blood of patriots & tyrants."[8] Peace requires the presence of armed conflict in order to be strengthened: civilization grows only within a constantly threatening barbarism that is as indispensable to it as oxygen.

As for *Finally*, it too is laden with ambivalence, like a suspended accusation: like a scandal revealed decades after the fact, a genocide finally called by its true name, evil finally laid bare, a long legal battle finally won. Finally, this marvellous novelist's talent is recognized, this dissident is celebrated as he ought to be, this position in my company that I have so much desired is finally mine. But this *Finally* is often a *Too Late*: it is the bitterness of belated rewards that they double the injury done the person who benefits from them. He has been ignored throughout his life, and when he is honored at a canonical age he's no longer interested in honors; they give him no pleasure. They should have thought of that earlier! Like a suitor who is accepted after years of assiduous courtship and rejections on the part of his idol, and who changes sides: it's no longer time; he has languished too long. Thus Frédéric Moreau, in Flaubert's *Sentimental Education*, encounters Madame Arnoux, with whom he had been madly in love. Sixteen years later, she rushes toward him, out of the blue. She seems on the point of offering herself to him, and is taking off her bonnet when the lamp suddenly illuminates her hair: it has gone white. "It was like a blow in the stomach."[9] He no longer dares touch her, repulsed by a vague dread of incest. The charm has been broken. They separate.

We are therefore rarely contemporary with what we experience. Dissonance is our mortal lot. There are authors, artists, film makers and inventors who are in the wrong period, no matter what their talent, and who fail to establish themselves in the same time zone as their compatriots. The *Zeitgeist*, the spirit of the time, has escaped them. They remain forever out of step. Their words, their productions resound in the void; they're not in sync. For their admirers, their work never reached the peak that would have allowed them to make it last. Ten years earlier or ten years afterward, they would have been acclaimed. They missed the right moment. History is cruel toward those in politics, philosophy, the sciences or the business world who have begun at the wrong time, not been recognized, failed in their careers, lost the war for fame and glory.

Kairos, the god of timeliness

The Greeks called *kairos* the propitious moment when one must act, between the too early and the too late, the art of slipping into the interstices of time. They represented Kairos, the god of opportunity, as a young man with a tuft of hair on his head. When he passes close to us, three possibilities arise: we don't see him; we see him and don't do anything; or we seize him by the hair and take control of him. We have to know how to seize the right time by the topknot, even at the risk of crashing in a temporal dead end if we are mistaken. Only a man or woman of action, aided by intuition, is able to seize the moment and never let it go, leaving all rivals far behind, sheepish. The latter understood the event badly, whereas the former discerned what everyone else saw without seeing it, seizing the occasion as a tiger seizes its prey. Luck is always a choice, the wager of grasping the hand held out by chance. In the same way, witty people have the genius of the retort, while others suffer from the *esprit de l'escalier*, the brilliant reply that occurs to them only when it is too late. The art of immediate decision is characteristic of great politicians, great generals, CEOs and surgeons, who are capable of coming up with a response on the spur of the moment, of reversing a defeat, of making decisions amid social chaos, in an economic crisis or when there is a serious injury. But it is also the talent of the pianist who improvises, electrified by chance, a sort of quicksilver capable of intercepting a few notes on the fly and transforming a musical phrase into sumptuous chords.

There is a difference between people who take advantage of a precise circumstance to make, in haste, a good decision and simple opportunists who let themselves drift in accord with situations, like a wisp of straw floating on the river's current. A great question for the worried activist: am I missing something? Shouldn't I go down into the street right now, spend the whole night out, grab any opportunity that comes along? Even death is governed by this logic: one has to know when to die – neither too soon nor too late. Woe to him who dies during a historical event or even at the same time as another celebrity, a famous singer, for example. He will be eclipsed. Jean Cocteau died at the same time as his friend Édith Piaf, and Jean d'Ormesson died twenty-four hours before Johnny Hallyday, who was awarded the honor of a national funeral; the American actress Farrah Fawcett died the same day as Michael Jackson and was swept aside in the whirlwind of that worldwide event. Contrary to the commonplace, the Grim Reaper is not egalitarian; he's a snob dependent on chance and public opinion.

Among the temporal adverbs that punctuate our lives, two stand out on equal terms: *Already* and *Still*. *Already* marks, for elders, a statistical anomaly, an irritating precociousness: already on the faculty, already a doctor, already a graduate at the age of twenty, already married, already a father? (Stupefaction at the hospital to be examined by a doctor the age of our children.) Already endowed with a biography as long as my arm, with worldwide fame when you've hardly emerged from adolescence? Already a blogger, an influential figure, famous on Instagram, a starlet? Precociousness is a pathology in the same way as senility is: a child shouldn't play the learned ape and a young man shouldn't disguise himself as a mature gentleman; nor should an old man sport gewgaws or deck himself out like a teenager. Go neither too fast, at the risk of cutting corners, nor regress, falling back into kid stuff.

Still marks an annoyance, a chronological anomaly: still traveling, still active, still in good shape? Still a night owl, still a clown at the age of fifty? If *already* notes an aptitude rare among young people, *still* marks an embarrassing persistence and really means: still there, still on the go? It also signals a discreet request; one more time, just one last time, the dying man says, asking that he be kept alive. One last trip to the seaside, a final visit to a great landscape, a masterpiece. One more dance before the curtain goes down. One more life to live!

On the blank page of your future lives[10]

In Book 10 of the *Republic*, Plato tells us, through a myth, how a young man named Er, having been found dead on the battlefield, wakes up at the moment of his cremation and describes his stay in the realm of the dead. In this immaterial world, souls are offered an opportunity to be reborn to mortal life by drawing lots according to their merits or faults in their former lives. There are more lives available, even animal lives, than there are candidates:[11] lives of tyrants, lives of rich or poor people, but most of the souls, lost, make their choices based on the happinesses or setbacks in their preceding lives, and some even prefer to be reincarnated in the form of a swan, a nightingale or an eagle. Similarly, animals take the form of humans or of different animals, the unjust in wild species, the just in tame species; in this way, mixtures of all kinds are made. Then the souls, passing under the throne of the goddess Necessity, drank from the River Ameles (carelessness) on the plain of Oblivion, lost the memory of what happened to them, and finally descended once more to earth.

That is why, in Plato, wise men practice anamnesis, the recollection of the idea formerly contemplated: we learn nothing new, we remember an ancient knowledge that lies buried in our consciousness and that our passage through the plain of Oblivion has made us forget. The reconquest of that lost knowledge is the task of the philosopher and marks his slow exit from the cave of ignorance. Marcel Proust was to return to this idea by comparing the resurrection of souls after death "to a phenomenon of memory."[12] It is our earlier lives that are recalled to us and flow in through the magic of a sensation. Proust himself inadvertently resuscitated many of his dead heroes in the course of the narrative and found them living again in later volumes. He did not want to separate himself from the family of his characters.[13]

How would we react if an evil genius said to us: you have the right to another new existence? Do you want it to be virtuous, mediocre or heroic? It's up to you to choose. How could we decide to choose a new cycle, with its inevitable disillusions, knowing what we already know? A science fiction writer, Philip José Farmer, no doubt inspired by Plato, hypothesizes that one day, after a great shout, all the humans who have died since the beginning of humanity awaken, naked and hairless, on the banks of an immense river, the *River of Eternity*.[14] Thirty to forty billion persons, most of them anonymous, but also including a few celebrities, among them Hermann Goering, Mark Twain, Jesus, Robert Burton (the English writer, 1577–1640) and Cyrano de Bergerac (the author who lived from 1619 to 1655), find themselves together, uncertain about the status of this adventure. A *Church of the Second Chance* offers them an opportunity to reorient their spiritual soul to become demi-gods. This utopia of the total recapitulation of the history of humanity overflows the simple planet earth and presupposes an expanding planet much larger than our own. But above all it implies bursts of deaths and resurrections in which humans emerge "from the waters of a lake as if from a uterus" because they are all registered on a matrix that causes them to undergo a biological treatment to repair and rejuvenate them. Assembly-line Resurrection, one might call it. It is impossible to escape the cycle of reincarnations: the Church of the Second Chance sees to it that, until the end of time, these multitudes are mixed so that a new human can appear, finally unburdened of all the imperfections of the old one.

While waiting for this hypothetical fiction, we poor mortals have to have a life in which the *Agains* come in at least a head before the *Too Lates*. There comes a time, after sixty, when another temporal imperative emerges: then, it's now or never! The grayness of dusk, the sweetness of memories do not prevent the morning desire to start out again on the right foot. We will not have a second or a third chance. There comes a time when it is *too late for the Too Late*.

FAMILY PHOTOS

A day comes when childhood, our childhood, appears to us quintessentially foreign: we hardly recognize the little kid we used to be, and there is something grotesque about his juxtaposition with today's adult. Like an unfortunate zigzag, as if a mad sculptor had bent our nose, lengthened our ears and, with a clumsy blow of his chisel, hollowed out our cheeks and stretched the skin over the bones. By what bizarre twist, of all the possible faces, did I inherit the one I have today? A mask of sagging skin and wrinkles! No logic, only a cruel accident that I am forced to accept. What is a family photo, from grandchildren to grandparents? A cruel tale that tells us: here's what's going to happen to you. Pretty faces will be creased, hair will fall out, figures will be deformed to the point of being unrecognizable. In these pictures, the young seem to be snatched by the oldest, literally vampirized as if time's arrow went only in the direction of withering. The dashing young man will grow stout like his father, the dreamy young woman will end up an old bag like her mother. A niece reminds you of your mother; by an ironic short-cut, a nephew has become the spitting image of his great-uncle. The old vampirize the young, imprint on them their pitiless mark. For stars, fate is even crueller: the last photos literally trample on those of their heyday. Simone Signoret, Elizabeth Taylor, destroyed by alcohol, or Antonin Artaud, toothless and grimacing, are forever marked by their image at the end of their lives. The only exceptions: the photographic resurrection of the dead. Steve McQueen posing forever for Breitling brand watches, Alain Delon for Christian Dior, seem frozen in their youth for all eternity. Like mummies on glossy paper, embalmed in their myth. We can also reanimate dead stars by hologram: Marilyn Monroe, Billie Holiday, the rapper Tupac Shakur go on tour with Frank Zappa and Claude François.

The law of generalized physical collapse has some fine exceptions: if certain people fade prematurely and become unrecognizable by the age of thirty, others mature elegantly and dominate their lineage from the height of their experience. Age has not made them more attractive, it has made them better; it has ennobled them. There are handsome, magnificent old people. They are the aristocrats of time.

A great question for the Fathers of the Church: at the time of the Last Judgment, which body will be resurrected, that of our radiant age or that of our decrepitude? Will we be given the choice of our preferred appearance? Will the infirm return with their handicaps, the martyrs with their tortures? St Thomas Aquinas devotes stupefying pages to this promise: "We are conceived in ignominy, we are reborn in glory, we are conceived in corruption, we are reborn in incorruptibility, we are conceived in weakness, we are reborn in strength, we are conceived as an animal body, we are reborn as a spiritual body." Then we will be transparent to the presence of God: men will remain men, women will remain women, and their genitals, now useless, will be maintained, as will their intestines, which will be filled with "noble humours," and their hair and nails, useful for adorning their appearance, on the condition that they are not too long. Blood and sperm will persist, but transfigured. Food will become useless, but it will remain possible to eat. Humankind will be dissolved in "the golden liquid of a spiritual body," incorruptible, enduring, immune to decay.[15] An extraordinary conception that recognizes the quasi-perfection of the human body, whose perishable character will at that time don the mantle of the imperishable. When the trumpet sounds the Last Judgment, the bodies will rise up. "Resuscitate means rise up." A splendid formula valid for all, whether one is a believer or not.

CHAPTER 8

Make a Success of One's Life, and Then What?

I still believe that life is not a problem to be solved but a risk to be taken, and, confronted by this total risk, the only competencies I know are love and saintliness.

GEORGES BERNANOS

We know Pindar's famous injunction "Become what you are," which complements this other formula peculiar to Antiquity: "Know yourself." This is a strange imperative: how can we become what we already are, except through artifice or violence?[1] For the Ancients, knowing oneself meant becoming aware of one's limits within the cosmos: each person, being only a microcosm within the macrocosm, must not exceed his own domain but, on the contrary, be governed by the course of the stars, avoiding the mortal sin of immoderation. For Moderns, inversely, ever since the Enlightenment, the self must happen by developing all of its faculties to avoid being stunted. That was already the meaning of the parable of the talents (both money and abilities) in the gospels of Luke and Matthew: a master gives five talents to his first servant, two to the second, and one to the third. The first brings him back ten, the second four, and the third returns to him the same talent, which he had hidden in the earth. The master rewards the first two servants and violently drives away the third, drawing this amazing conclusion: "For to every one who has will more be given, and he will have abundance; but from him who has not, even what he has will be taken away" (Matthew 25: 29). The philosophical moral of this parable is that we have to make the gifts given us by nature or by God bear fruit, on pain of sinning against the spirit. It is our merits that define us better than privileges of birth. But today this self-fulfillment no longer has to follow the traditional order or religious commandments: in an individualistic universe, it is produced by exploring oneself, even if that means abandoning the roles that social, family and clan conditioning imposes on us.

I am I, alas

Henceforth, authenticity – that is, conformity with the deep self – has to take priority over convention, sincerity over the social game, singularity over the collective. But the notion of authenticity is itself ambiguous.

   Is it a question of becoming what one is for all eternity, a predestined, programmed self that just has to manage to bloom and, once its goal has been attained, remain what it is? Which would mean that we shouldn't burden ourselves with any hindrance or guidance but listen only to our own exquisite subjectivity. Authenticity would be a modern, noble reformulation of the old word "caprice," the royal *bon plaisir*. Don't worry about reform or moral progress:

you're perfect just the way you are; cultivate your singularity, which is good simply because it is yours. Don't resist any inclination, because your desire is sovereign. Everyone has duties except you. That is all the ambivalence of the 1960s watchword: *be yourself*. And, to be yourself, being has to be able to happen; at fifteen you can't be all that you will someday be able to be.

Given to myself, all I have to do is glorify myself unreservedly: the supreme value is no longer what transcends me but what I observe in myself. I no longer "become," I am all that I must be at every moment; I can adhere without remorse to my character, my emotions, my fantasies. Whereas liberty is the faculty of freeing oneself from determinism, we claim to espouse it as closely as possible (and the same thing happens in identity politics: each minority has to keep to itself in the perfection of what it is and not move outside the circle of like-minded people). No limit is set to our appetites; we no longer need to construct ourselves – that is, to introduce a distance within the self. Each of us has only to follow his own inclination, to fuse with himself. A strange indulgence that affects both the democratic individual and communities very full of themselves, when they have a feeling that the world owes them everything.

It remains that we always end up becoming something that we call, in a rather facile manner, "oneself." *To the comfort of being oneself is added the malaise of being nothing but oneself.* We have constructed ourselves, and now we would like to reconstruct or deconstruct ourselves. It is here that age may introduce a little clear-sightedness into this proclamation of the self as the absolute model. "Know yourself," said the Greek oracle, in order to know your limits and your potentialities. But there's only me in me, alas, whatever I do, and I need a little more than my being to exist. It doesn't take long to make the rounds of that property-owner. What happens when one has become what one is, when one knows or misjudges oneself? "I don't know what I am, I'm not what I know," said the German mystic Angelus Silesius (1624–1677). Freud added: I am not the one I think I am, the self is not master in its own house, it is moved by the great forces of the unconscious and the Superego, the whirlwind of appetites and tribunal of censorship. Well and good; but that does not make each of us a great Other or a being of amazing profundity and foreignness. Even if psychoanalysis often gives patients the fascinating feeling that they are soaring above the abysses of their innermost selves.

The risk is not only that of taking oneself to be someone, and the frequent good fortune to succeed in doing so (Chateaubriand and Victor Hugo provide good examples), but also that of imprisoning oneself in one's splendid uniqueness, of reproducing ad infinitum the same figure. Isn't it more exciting to proclaim: be what you aren't? *We spend half a century finding ourselves; afterward we are dying to lose ourselves a little.* If each of us is several, which characters appear in the last act? It's possible that immaturity prolonged beyond the permissible dates is also an asset, a way of remaining in a state of astonishment with regard to the world until an advanced age. Youth: all of us, or at least most, want to be honorary citizens of that country that we lost long ago. "I still feel young," say people in their forties, fifties and even sixties, and they may be right in their childish revolt against the obvious. "Forty," said Péguy, "is a terrible age, an unpardonable age ... It no longer tolerates being deceived ... because it is the age when we become what we are."[2] A fatal vision that resounds like a guillotine: people in their forties are incarcerated in their temporal framework without any chance of escaping from it. Alone, in a tête-à-tête with ourselves, we quickly come to feel like an unwelcome intruder. Then it is urgent not to remain encumbered by one's person, to blend into action, work or love. There is nothing terrible or irremediable in this, to borrow Péguy's formula, except that, in his time, the forties were already on the brink of old age. But, today, people in their forties are nearly virginal with regard to life and still have enough resources to change and surprise themselves. Care for the self, advocated so strongly by Michel Foucault at the end of his career, is legitimate in the periods of education, the apprenticeship years. Later, it is related to laziness or to prudent safeguarding. Producing oneself as a subject also implies that one is trying to escape this imperative.

Rousseau drew a luminous distinction between *amour de soi*, self-love, which is positive, and *amour propre*, vanity, which arises from competition and comparison with others. There is a third, uneasy kind of self-love that has developed with vulgarized Freudianism and that transforms each human being into a little package of problems and tensions that is regularly laid at the feet of others or of one's analyst.[3] This is a narrative register that comes from the Christian confession, the self-examination *that transforms the minuscule into a thrilling adventure*: everything makes sense, everything deserves to be noted, there is no waste; you have to dissect yourself, associate endlessly. We know those individuals who are completely self-absorbed, fascinated by their little troubles. (And the very definition of unhappiness is never being able to escape from oneself.) They never forget themselves, and, no matter where they go or what they do, they fall back into their ruts. They think they are endowed with an inexhaustible psyche and comment on their slightest lapses, their slightest slips of the tongue, as if they were high deeds. Commentary is their curse; they never stop deciphering themselves like an unfathomable enigma. The dizzying abyss called the self captivates them. But that abyss is also a hell that prevents them from ever getting out of themselves and leaves them riveted to their shell.

Opening up to what is not oneself is not reducible to caprice or inconstancy. Sartre recognized ironically in *The Words* that he had constructed himself on "the noble mandate to be unfaithful to everything."[4] This infidelity to himself is never more than another form of loyalty, as an adulterous lover remains constant in his conjugal cheating. It's the dream of a controlled dispossession: becoming another person without ceasing to be the one you are. Long before Sartre, Gide had cried, with a touch of dandyism: "Future, how much I'd like you to be unfaithful," and he asked his reader to leap "to the other extremity of his self." But this other extremity is still us: we want to flee ourselves, but we remain attached no matter what we say. This aspiration to change our personality can resemble a thirst for novelty or a programmed betrayal: a desire to move with our period, even to disavow ourselves when we have gone astray. But a traitor is still loyal only to himself. He wants to slip away from himself without discarding himself. The apostate repudiates himself less than he remains faithful to a lofty idea of himself through successive commitments. His reversals are often continuities.

The three faces of freedom

The human adventure's lack of meaning is the very condition of freedom and at the same time its curse. It forces us to discover it in ourselves, in half-light and indecisiveness. We make our way through a labyrinth of errors and dead ends in which bright intervals sometimes occur. As soon as we think we are saved, another peril arises. Freedom, our ability to lead our lives as we see fit, has at least three stages, which are not always consecutive: revolt, constraint and solitude. When we emerge from childhood, freedom is first manifested by rebellion against family, teachers, the established order. We want to develop without guidance, to test our strength. I am my own master, cries the teenager who has received the benefits of education and wants to throw off his chains. Then comes the recognition that freedom also entails responsibility, that it obliges us to accept the consequences of our acts. I have to answer for myself without seeking to escape: we are never free except in a straitjacket that limits us and defines us at the same time. A time that is as demanding as it is dazzling. The price to be paid for the right to speak in the first person, to say "I," is an existential solitude that can border on despair. I suffer alone, I will die alone, encumbered by myself, forever a prisoner of the body that has been given me, of the history I have lived. That is the dark side of our autonomy. Who can I blame when I suffer, when I'm going nowhere, when I fail, if I myself am my sole obstacle? Only the emancipation is glorious; once acquired, freedom is always disappointing.

So it is tempting to try to get round freedom, to speak rather of liberation without end and to prolong adolescent rebellion as far as possible. As if we were, at thirty or forty, still under the control of our parents, of society, which we can blame for all our difficulties. Because innocence evaporates at the same time as our cheeks lose their plumpness and peach-fuzz, a day comes when I become truly responsible for my acts without being able to blame them on anyone else. I have to prove myself and I will be judged in accord with them. It is the misfortune and the marvel of growing up, of becoming an adult. Hence we constantly work out compromises between insubordination and requests for help: take care of me when I'm feeling bad, leave me alone when I'm feeling good. It is the sweetness of our democratic societies that they attenuate the citizen's isolation through the exercise of solidarity. Solidarity protects our rights and lightens the brutality of our difficulties.

The meaning of life is thus a question that survives all the answers given. A time comes when we have to stop asking "Who am I?" and ask instead "What can I do?" What am I allowed to undertake at this point in my life? To escape oneself, one has to remember that "the shortest way to get from us to us is the universe" (Malcolm de Chazal). The richness of a destiny is always connected with the encounters that have punctuated it, and without which each of us would have no depth. Getting old means honoring an endless promissory note; we are composed of all these others that we have encountered – *each of us is a collective work that says "I."*

Many people, we know, force themselves to be what they are not or hide their true nature (in the register of sexual orientation, for example). They are happy to convert to themselves (Seneca), to return to themselves as if to a haven of peace sheltered from the storms of the world. Finding oneself, finding one's way: that is the first stage in a reconciliation with oneself. It is the marvellous moment when we become the masters of our own destiny. We cease to be commanded from outside, we act by ourselves. Happy are those who know very early on what suits them and do not get lost in tergiversations and digressions. In the old days, in the Western world, converting to oneself entailed renouncing one's real being, either by submitting to divine law or by obeying a master or a morality.[5] People conformed to a social order at the price of repressing their true vocation. To want to change one's life, it is already necessary to think that it belongs to you rather than to God, the Church, the synagogue, the mosque, your community, or the social class you came from. That presupposes not only a loosening of tribal, clan or traditional ties but also the certainty that change, from one generation to another, is preferable to stability. According to the credo of the Enlightenment, to grow up, to reach maturity, is to pass from the heteronomy of childhood, where I remain under surveillance, to the autonomy of maturity, where I am expected to give myself my own law.

The desire to have a life of one's own, and not a uniform borrowed from social conventions, from others, is an aspiration that has emerged only recently in history. In particular, it is an American promise: that everyone will write the scenario for his own destiny as he wishes. An ambiguous promise, to be sure, because it is compromised by social inequalities and discriminations of all kinds. The Old World, rooted in an aristocratic past, long resisted this injunction. "You come along, you find a life, ready-made, you only have to put it on,"[6] wrote Rilke in Paris in the early twentieth century. Even the desire to have a death of one's own, he noted, is becoming increasingly rare; everyone is "happy if they find one that more or less fits." It is because we are free that we have a destiny. Alienated people don't have a destiny; they have only a common direction – they head by compact groups toward the same destination. The democratic individual rebels against that submissiveness. He would like to be the sole owner of himself. But this self-enjoyment, this pleasure taken in being lord over one's lands, does not prevent us from remaining sensitive to the fortunate accidents that chance brings us: to entertain, for example, a dream of dispossession of which love would be the most perfect illustration, because loving is first of all not belonging to oneself, consenting voluntarily to being dispossessed of ourselves.

A door opening on the unknown

At any age, living well might be summed up in a twofold commandment: once the right formula is found, don't change, but remain prepared to respond to the beauties of the world. Without repudiating oneself, one can want the future to have a surprising face, not that of satiation but, rather, the more likeable one of the unexpected. The simple fact of sensing, while still young, that we have a more favorable destiny often allows us to tear down the walls that imprison us. The charm of departures, of ruptures, is that they throw us into the unknown and tear a beneficial rip in the fabric of time. To the pleasure and reality principles we must add a third, the principle of the Outside, insofar as it is the realm of diversity, of the inexhaustible savor of things. The elsewhere, the foreign, is often the site of revelation.

Sometimes, in the course of a journey or a fortuitous accident, we are granted the intuition of other, shattering worlds: like Flaubert's Pécuchet, who is galvanized by a splendidly indecent peasant girl whose pleasures behind a hedge he witnesses, causing him to question, for a moment, his vocation as a frantic copyist. Is it surprising that this appeal to mystery is predominant especially in the three domains of religion, eroticism and travel, the three sites of human transcendence, the appeal to the flesh, the appeal to God and the appeal to other continents? We have to have passed through this door opening on the unexplored at least once in our lives. It is the door of the sacred: everything depends on the imminence of a leap, comparable to a religious conversion, that frees us from ourselves, from the asphyxiating powers of routine. The unexpected is the secular version of salvation.

The fact that the future is aleatory – that is, marked by plasticity – is the chance that something unprecedented might happen to us, even if in the very last years of life. This feverish desire to confront the high seas of adventure never dissipates. At any time, it should be possible to sail off to other destinies. But at this risk: that someone who has shuffled along in routine tasks for thirty years might set out, in a burst of last-minute heroism, on a hazardous enterprise for which he is not prepared. We have too many examples of people in their fifties, both men and women, sedentary and overweight, who throw themselves into extreme sports overnight and end up in the emergency room. The senior citizen who suddenly takes himself for an aerialist and decides to go bungee-jumping, the retiree who disguises herself as a fighter and goes off to sink into the sands of some remote desert, the ancestor who thinks he's a Casanova and gets taken to the cleaners by clever young women are well-known figures in comedy. Not everything is possible at all ages, and there is also a propriety regarding physical abilities. In his *Diary of a Country Priest*, Bernanos speaks of the men brought to light by the war and who, without it, would have remained mere "stumps of men."[7] Thank God, we don't need a war to reach the light. At each stage, it remains possible to proceed to analyze metaphorically the old man (or the old woman).

Perhaps, to prevent the soul from getting rusty, it is necessary to lodge one's best enemy within oneself, in accord with a precept in the gospels, the fertile and not the sterile *daimon*. Learn to become one's own best adversary, the one who wakes you up and stimulates you with his goad. That might be the secret of a good life: to cultivate the proper division that gets you going and forces you to move forward with a slight but fertile limp.

"I'm afraid that, if my demons go, my angels will go with them" (Rainier Maria Rilke).

Succeed, but not entirely

What happens once we have succeeded in life?[8] Will we rest on our laurels, expect others to weave our crowns, cover our chests with medals and tinkling baubles, managing our success as if it were an inheritance? A fascinating question about the last years of great captains of industry, researchers, mathematicians, seafarers and artists, male or female, who have arrived at the peak of their glory and are forced to live on, in spite of everything, as parasites or as witnesses to their work, which rejects them after using them.[9] Every successful life, if there is such a thing, escapes the logic of a positive or negative balance. It is no more than a series of challenges and defeats surmounted and of unspeakable shames that form its dark side. Is life a summit that we finish climbing around the age of fifty, after which we descend again toward the flatland, admiring the twilight? The metaphor is tempting, but it's only a metaphor. To mature is often to undertake a melancholic inventory of everything we have not achieved. But this melancholy suggests negatively a vast domain to be cultivated: everything that remains for us to explore.

Ideally, a successful life makes all the desirable goals converge toward a determinate totality, toward what the Greeks called excellence, a form of perfection in a precise domain. Sometimes a life that is coming to an end complies with the principle of condensation: completing in a few years everything we had neglected earlier. No one can define, at the risk of falling into vague generalities, precisely what a successful life is, but *everyone knows instinctively what a bad or ugly life is*. A great question in education as well as in politics: how can we avoid the rancor, the inexpiable hatreds, how can we recover from a failure, so we don't have to say, like a character of Zweig's:

"In me, there is always a defeated man who wants to take revenge."[10] Perhaps we should speak instead of *a fulfilled life*: a life that is open to the disturbance of the unforeseen, escapes the obligation of drawing up a balance sheet and commits a future power, even if it is nearing its end. The concept of success is awkward insofar as it seems to conclude the quest, since the most desirable state has been attained as if the adventure were over.

There is a great pride, tinged with melancholy, in having accomplished one's objectives, fulfilled one's mission. That is the sweet sorrow of a life that has ceased to wander because it thinks it has found its harbor and is henceforth dedicated to staying where it is. Odysseus must have been unhappy once he had returned home, as the great Greek poet Constantin Cavafy (1863–1933) suggested, wishing that Odysseus might reach Ithaca as late as possible:

> But don't hurry the journey at all.
> Better if it lasts for years,
> so you are old by the time you reach the island,
> wealthy with all you have gained on the way,
> not expecting Ithaka to make you rich.[11]

The return itself should never be anything but a stopover. Our desire's most cherished object has value only if it remains inaccessible and especially unknown: it is the movement that we prize more than the objective; it is remaining mobile that makes us alive. Some people strive to avoid complete success in their domain in order to leave themselves a future and not bar its way. (Like wealthy people who bankrupt themselves almost voluntarily in order to repeat the exciting adventure of getting rich.) The gospels say that God wants to be sought, not to find him but to continue to search for him.

Thus all we can do is fail, try, fail again, try, fail better, as Samuel Beckett put it. How can truth emerge from error, from an incessant correction of the setbacks through which we have gone? Even when we have arrived at an honorable age we are still not entirely what we could be. There is a certain weariness in being attached to oneself like an oyster to its rock, and a beauty in leaving oneself behind a little, in being tested by novelty or alterity. Who could enrich me, connect me with something greater than I? What a misfortune to have only one life, only one body, only one identity, only one sex, instead of being plural, able to embody oneself at will in the countless possible destinies that surround us. I would so much like to be reborn as a woman, a Hindu, a South American, a man of the Middle Ages, the Renaissance, the Mayan Empire, or even as a wolf, a bear or a songbird, to experience an endless process of metempsychosis!

Not everything is possible

A happy life is not only an "adolescent dream realized in maturity" (Alfred de Vigny, *Cinq-Mars*), it is also a destiny that has joined itself to something vaster, opened itself up to a certain dimension. Existence here on earth is perfect in each of its moments and to be perfected at every one of them. On the condition that the potential is distinguished from the possible. The potential is crucial in adolescence, when it is a matter of deploying one's talents, making demands on one's faculties through work and learning. This is an internal development that is indispensable for everyone. We come into our own through labor and knowledge. The possible belongs to a different order: external to the self, it is a compromise between the world and my aspirations and unveils in all of us unknown

147

aspects that force us to transcend ourselves. I realize myself through my abilities, I get ahead of myself, I re-create myself through the things I experience. That is revealed by the expression "I'd never have thought myself capable of doing that." With the possible, we pass from governing the self to broadening its being by means of reality.

Let's not delude ourselves with crazy hopes: starting at a certain age, we can no longer put our lives on the line as we would cast another die, do anything at all, go into biological research, automobile racing, parachuting, mathematics. At sixty, it is even less true than it was at twenty that the sky is the limit. That is the American "can do" attitude, which sets no limit to the abilities of an individual provided that he rolls up his sleeves – the optimism of a pioneer nation that believes in the marriage of efficiency and will. We cannot – less than ever – escape the necessity of making choices and abandon ourselves to the intoxication of the unlimited. Age reduces uncertainties. But constraints, by restricting us, also strengthen our freedom.

Nonetheless, we remain, in certain privileged moments, overwhelmed by urges, appetites, dreams so rich that we are incapable of sorting them out, stunned by their multitude. It is an intoxication that can paralyze us, analogous to the dizziness of the teenager who sees all roads opening up to him. "The real is narrow, the possible is immense," as Henri-Frédéric Amiel put it in his *Journal*: throughout his life, this nineteenth-century Swiss man of private means suffered from abulia and experienced nothing for lack of the ability to embrace all directions. At every age, new potentialities await us in this world. What one can expect from undergoing psychoanalysis, Freud said, was to be reconciled not with reality but rather with one's own abilities. To want what one wants, to be able to do what one can. Not to want what one can, grovelling before reality. Nor to be able to do what one wants – to believe it – a figure of omnipotence. But that one can play one's part, tell one's story, respond to the world in one's own way. Love and work.[12]

Such is the Indian summer of life: the reconquest of lost possibilities even if the field of virtualities gets smaller every day. We must remain an open consciousness that allows itself to be moved and affected, without ever being satiated. Referring to a little café-au-lait seller, whose face is "flushed by the reflections of the morning sun ... rosier than the sky," and who is walking alongside a train that has stopped at a station for the awakened passengers, Marcel Proust writes: "I felt in her presence that desire to live which is reborn in us whenever we become conscious anew of beauty and of happiness."[13] The savor of the passing days resides in this very simple but very important thing: not knowing what one is going to find, discovering new pathways, not being constantly brought back to oneself. That is *the grandeur of interruption*, the dream of escape. What better can we hope for in life? Splendid events, splendid meetings with exceptional people who raise us above ourselves. And who offer us the grace of a visit. The prayer of the mature man or woman: Lord, grant me a last blaze of love, of contemplation, before extinction; a new birth late in life so that my last years may be illuminated, in addition to all the pleasures that destiny has granted me. A "successful" life is an existence in a state of perpetual rebirth, in which the ability to begin over again wins out over the established and acquires the power of an uninterrupted surge.[14] We have both to be content with what the world offers us and demand more from it, accentuate in it the expectation of a wonder, of a whirlwind. An existence is all the richer the greater the gap between its point of departure and its point of arrival: being born in a ghetto and ending up as a great artist, like, for example, the musician and producer Quincy Jones. There's always an elegant way of getting around fate, even if ultimately no one escapes the irreparable.

The quest for a captivating life must obey two contradictory injunctions: being fully satisfied with our fate while also remaining attentive to the murmuring of the world, to the little music of foreign things. Immersion in the marvellous today, availability to wonders from outside. *The happiness of continuity, the happiness of suspense,* the happiness of contraction, on the one hand, and the happiness of dilation on the other, serenity and intoxication, the same old story and escape. It's only the contrast between the one and the other that generates exhilaration.

TRANSMISSION DESPITE MISUNDERSTANDING

In a democracy, said de Tocqueville, each generation is a new nation and tradition is less an imperative than a source of information. Transmitting has become a problematic task: the temptation is great for older people to kneel down before their juniors for fear of being declared worthless, as Plato already indicated in his *Republic*. But to concede everything to the newcomers, brusquely sweeping away the heritage of which one is the bearer, is not to help them but, rather, to keep them in the prison of the present, to incarcerate them in the pure actuality of which they are the mirror and the echo. Then one ceases to be a teacher of maturity and becomes a teacher of prostration. Instead of learning the necessity of the long term, one becomes the servile courtier of youth and the present moment. The mentor is transformed into a lackey, the tutor into a sycophant.

A stereotype suggests that we are experiencing the inversion of the educational relationship caused by technological innovation. Children are said to become the parents of their parents and teach them, day after day, the rudiments of the internet. They are supposed to be "digital natives" (Nicholas Negroponte) who are de-legitimizing the reputation for knowledge and wisdom that is wrongly attributed to adults. "What matters will no longer be membership in this or that class, whether social, racial or economic, but in the right generation. The rich people are now the young, and the impoverished are the old."[15] From now on, it's up to children to educate their parents and to adapt them, like the sons and daughters of immigrants, to the new global environment. "You're too cool for school," said, it seems, Jeff Bezos and Steve Jobs (schools produce nothing but robots). But universal accessibility to all kinds of knowledge has nothing to do with initiation into a demanding discipline. Clicking on "astrophysics" or "organic chemistry" doesn't make people astrophysicists or chemists, or even popularizers – just illiterate pedants. The democracy of the click is nothing but a democracy of ignoramuses. A scientist is not merely a dilettante who has succeeded; he has worked his whole life on the same subjects. We are abandoning these illusions, especially now that many great figures in Silicon Valley are forbidding their own children to use iPads, tablets and other computers that harm concentration and creativity. Knowing and know-how should not be confused; young people's dexterity is a technical feat, not a symbolic superiority.[16] Although our duty, as elders, is in fact to teach the past, to resuscitate great figures now dead so that they remain alive alongside the other living, to exhume them from the earth where they slumber, we also have to master new tools, to avoid becoming alien to our own period, ghosts lost in a universe of signs that we no longer understand. Old people's electronic illiteracy deprives them of any means of surviving in the modern bureaucratic labyrinth. They are trying to get their bearings in innovations the way we look for the right frequency on a radio.

Starting at a certain age, we all become immigrants in time. The old forms of snobbery no longer work, reflexes have changed, the demotic is misleading; we have a desperate need for mediators and translators to convert the particular dialects into a common language. It is through words that we are dated and socially situated. We have to relearn young people's customs, incorporate their new expressions, keep up with the current taste, on pain of no longer "being with it, pop," as people said in the 1960s. The eagerness with which we pick up the slang of the high schools and housing projects, as if we were learning a foreign language, is accompanied by hesitancy to use it, except between scare quotes, for fear of seeming ridiculous. Every age group has its semantic totems, its obsolete swear words, its outdated expressions that grow old with it except when they are inventive or curious enough to be considered worthy of entering into the common lexicon. Our language itself deposits in its utterances each decade's fashions and tics, which resurface like the alluvia of a river.

The error made by adults is to believe that what they know is known to everyone, whereas knowledge is not a uniform mass that moves at the same pace for all humanity. Reference points have changed, the great historical dates no longer refer to the same affects. In each case our disciplines have to be patiently reconverted into a common idiom without vulgarizing or degrading them, using a strategy of intuitive desynchronization. We need a temporal GPS and a radio to put us and the others on the same wavelength. If "words die of thirst," as Octavio Paz said, the best way to quench that thirst is to make them desirable once again to those who are not only ignorant of them but do not even suspect that they might exist.

The past is a treasure that we must resuscitate to prevent those who succeed us from being deprived of it. Giving them the keys to the world is not to ask them to imitate us but rather to enable them to challenge us, in full knowledge of the facts. They may turn this freedom against us, as when Caliban says: "You taught me language, and my profit on't / Is I know how to curse." What matters is being able to say: the connection is established, the transmission has been made. Provided that what is communicated to them is not only disgust with life and with the human race, like the message of so many prophets of doom these days. Each generation can play only a precise historical role, after which it has to yield to the next. It is a link in a long chain that has preceded it and will survive it. It is said that Fred Astaire (1899–1987), who met Michael Jackson on several occasions, inspired him and helped him make the clip of the song "Thriller" (1982), sent him this telegram: "I'm an old man. I was waiting for my replacement. Thanks."[17] The good teacher has to agree to disappear once his work is done.

PART V

What Does Not Die in Us

CHAPTER 9

Death, Where is Thy Victory?

All men are mortal; but for each man his death is an accident and, even if he knows that and consents to it, an undue violence.

SIMONE DE BEAUVOIR

Monsieur Seguin's Goat

Every story for children can be read in at least two ways, the first edifying, for pedagogical purposes, and another more subtle and occasionally hidden. Take Alphonse Daudet's *Monsieur Seguin's Goat*: it appears to be an apologue about disobedience. Monsieur Seguin is a herdsman who lives in Provence; he has no goats because all of them, one after another, attracted by the wide-open spaces, have gone off and been eaten by the wolf. When he buys a goat named Blanquette, she, too, languishes and tries to escape. He closes her up in a stable, but she succeeds in getting out through an opening in the wall. In her turn, she goes to gambol on the mountainside, intoxicated by her freedom, and feasts, alongside chamois, on tasty grasses. When dusk comes, she shivers; the wolf has just appeared in the high grass and is staring at her calmly. She fights him all night long, her horns lowered, but at dawn, exhausted and covered with blood, she lies down and lets herself be devoured.

Read to undisciplined children, this story seems to praise the rule: anyone who rebels against his parents or his teachers is risking the worst. Woe to the disobedient! But behind this bland moral there is another, richer one: as soon as a living being reaches adulthood, it enjoys its freedom until dusk, after which, even if it fights ferociously, death carries it off. Monsieur Seguin's goat doesn't surrender; it fights until it is exhausted, and this nocturnal battle constitutes all the richness of this tale. "One fights not to conquer evil but to prevent it from winning" (Seneca).

Can one resign oneself to death, make one's peace with it? No, because it continues, down to the end, to reduce us to dust, it is the "bitch" that gnaws on us and crumbles us (Guy de Maupassant).[1] It is not an enemy with which we could negotiate but an implacable law that constantly erodes, day after day, our vital process. We can only sign provisional truces. "Life is the totality of the forces that resist death," said the physiologist Marie François Xavier Bichat (1771–1802) in a phrase that has been plagiarized countless times. Even if some people contest the accuracy of the definition,[2] it remains eloquent. We die every day in each of the hours that are granted us, and the last one will succeed in killing us. Life is born from the ongoing repression of cellular suicide, *apoptosis* (Jean-Claude Ameisen),[3] that prevents the organism from destroying itself. To exist, Proust already said, is to resist the fragmentary and successive deaths that permeate the whole duration of our lives.[4] Paraphrasing Bichat, we could similarly say: "Death is the totality of the forces that destroy life the better to resuscitate it." We will be obliterated so that others may rise up on earth in their turn.

Eternity in love with time

Our period intones a strange complaint: death is supposed to be in danger. We are headed for a shortage of deaths. "I fear that we might be the last generation to die," writes Gerald Jay Sussman, a professor at MIT and a specialist in artificial intelligence. With the despotism of an obsession that tolerates no rival, the battle against death has become the objective of the super-rich who want to escape the common lot, and especially that great equalizer, the Grim Reaper. "The devil take the physical body, it is of no interest," cries Hans Moravec, a specialist in robotics. "We all want to be immortal." Since it is the flesh and biological processes that will bring about our ruin, we have to move as quickly as possible toward a post-biological era, with thinking, complex, incorruptible robots that will allow us to replace the body with a bionic structure. "Clones, cyborgs and artificial organs are coalescing to give our humanity a new face."[5] The mind is supposed to be on the verge of triumphing over nature, of killing disease and death, which, once relegated to the antique shop, will render the birth of new generations superfluous. Billionaires are having very expensive crypts constructed to hold their brains so that, after the technological transition, they can be recuperated and reloaded on machines.

So now we have entered the era of ecstatic promises. On 6 October 2012, the urologist and surgeon Laurent Alexandre, a supporter of transhumanism, gave a talk in Paris in which he announced the impending demise of death. Our life expectancy having tripled over the past two hundred and fifty years, we are confronting, according to him, four scenarios: a drastic decrease in longevity because of pollution, a stagnation, a continued increase up to 120 or 150 years, or an exponential increase thanks to the qualitative leaps made possible by nanotechnologies, robotics and genetic engineering. He concluded his talk with this provocative proclamation (regarding which he has since changed his mind, with humility): "My conviction is that some of you in this room will live a thousand years."[6] A titanic battle was supposed to take place between silicon and neurons, to "interface" our brain with artificial intelligence. Not only would ageing be reversible, thanks to the procedure of "dechronification" – that is, cellular rejuvenation – but also the disappearance of death itself would be just a question of time. This detestable remnant of human pre-history would be part of the past as well. The essential point is to hold on until research succeeds in killing the monster. We know that an Italian neurosurgeon, Sergio Canavero, would like to graft heads onto new, alternative bodies, those of donors who are brain dead, like a hard disk being installed in a computer.

In 2011, the artist Orlan launched a petition on line, in English, against death:

> ENOUGH IS ENOUGH!
> It's been going on way too long!
> It must stop!
> I don't agree, I don't want to die!
> I don't want my friends to die!
> It's time to react against death.[7]

A British scientist, Aubrey de Grey, proposes to regenerate cellular tissues to extend life expectancy infinitely. He has created the Methuselah Foundation, to which rich donors contribute. The new demiurges of Silicon Valley, including Raymond Kurzweil and his Singularity University, are seeking to overcome death by throwing billions of dollars at it: it suffices to pay the price. "Death really makes me mad, it makes no sense," says Larry Ellison, the co-founder of the firm Oracle and the seventh richest man in the world.[8] For his part, John Unis, the head of an investment fund, said: "I wager that ageing is a code, a code that it will suffice to crack and pirate." Immortality, or rather amortality, is thus becoming the demand of the most well-off people, who are eager to hold this ultimate privilege.

Foreseeing the impending death of death (whereas others foresee the end of the world) leaves us perplexed for more reasons than one. These resounding predictions run a serious risk of aiming at the stars and ending up in the gutter, as Hegel said about erudition. Does the fact that living a thousand years may someday be possible for everyone make it desirable? Is stubbornly persisting in being, encumbering the planet with one's presence for centuries, really necessary? One cannot help thinking of Odysseus' paradox: taken in by the nymph Calypso after a shipwreck on his way back to Ithaca, he is cared for, fed and loved for seven years by his hostess, whose lover he becomes. Then Calypso proposes to make him immortal. But Odysseus, weeping on the seashore, dreams of returning to his family. Calypso is tiring him out, forcing him to make love to her every night. Even if his Penelope is not as splendid as the goddess, he wants to go home, to see his native land and people again. The attraction of the familiar is stronger than the seductiveness of the unknown. Zeus takes pity on Odysseus. He has Hermes order Calypso to let him leave: in four days, Odysseus constructs a raft, receives perfumes and abundant food from his hostess, sets out on the seas, survives another terrible storm, and finally makes it home.

161

This text can be read in at least two ways: despite his attraction to Calypso, Odysseus clearly shows his preference for a mortal, and thus limited, existence. As for Calypso, she cannot conceal, by becoming attached to him, that she is an immortal falling in love with a mortal, with the fleeting nature of life. What Homer tells us is of a disturbing profundity: the gods, who are destined to live forever, both invisible and omnipresent, are jealous of humans' mortality. Didn't Jesus himself, by making himself a man on earth, show his love of the Incarnation, testifying to the grandeur of eternity in time, but also to the value of time for those who are uncreated? The tears he shed on the cross were human tears. Replying to those who ask "What was God doing before he made heaven and earth?", St Augustine replies that the question is meaningless, since God, who created all times, cannot have made a time before time because, for Him, where there is no time, "there can be no then" or "never."[9] However, the question is not absurd. Officially, the Universe as we know it was created by the All-Powerful to make eternity desirable. What if it was the other way round – if God had invented the world out of weariness with his status? Didn't he fall in love with his creation, even as he urged his creatures to do all they could to join him in Paradise? And if his omnipotence was his weakness, if humans' duty was to help God die? It is the brevity of existence that is the true miracle, not the phantasmagorical constructions of religions promising us beatitude – that is, from our point of view, an endless dullness. The delights of Eden are less delicious than the fleeting destiny of humans. If there is an eternity, it is here and now, where we live.

The luck to die someday?

In the history of ideas, three forms of immortality are
generally distinguished: that of the people, for Jews; that
of the polis, for the Greeks; and that of the individual, for
Christians.[10] Our period has become attached to this last,
even though it favors an immortality without either god
or reconciliation, a simple unlimited duration. To be more
precise, it is a question of hyper-longevity, because even a
human who was a thousand years old would finally die. In
the Middle Ages, death was not the end of life; it was just
a transition toward the Creator. The terror of having to
confront God, to endure the possible punishment for one's
sins, was supposed to overshadow the fear of extinction.
The end was the narrow gate to salvation or damnation:
one lost one's meagre terrestrial goods, with the hope of
acquiring others that were more essential and would last
forever. Fear was attenuated by the prospect of redemption.

What is unique about the idea of eternity, and its
reinvention by Christianity, is that it accords each of us, no
matter how wretched, a place in the sun. The persistence
of my little person, beyond the terrestrial parenthesis, was
dazzling news. The simple fact of being born favors me
with a longevity that is potentially unlimited if I pass the
"test" of the Last Judgment. The test is attenuated, it is
true, by the long detour through Purgatory, that waiting
room for Salvation, where the souls of the dead bide their
time pending a decision regarding their fate. Another
brilliant invention: Christ died in his full glory, at the age
of thirty-three. An octogenarian, hoary Jesus would have
made a bad impression. While God the father is a solemn,
terrifying old man, the crucifixion of his son in the prime of
life is a magnificent narrative find. The gospels provided a
religious basis for the myth of eternal youth. The paradox of

Christianity: *to experience eternal life, you have to begin by dying*. Then God will weigh souls, intercessors will deliver their pleas, and the supreme Judge will hand down his decisions. Meaning is offered humans, along with a chance of being redeemed in the event that they stray. Death is a purification that makes it possible to distinguish the essential from the accessory. My advent on earth is no longer a mere accident; my contingent birth establishes me forever in the great family of the potentially resuscitated. Life on earth is a pilgrimage from the Fall to the Redemption.

As for profane immortality, which remains for the moment a hypothesis, it is not necessarily heartening. Some promises are akin to curses. In *Gulliver's Travels*, Jonathan Swift shows us his hero meeting a tribe of immortals, the Struldbruggs: they are lonely and unhappy because they are stripped of their civil rights when they reach the age of eighty and are reduced to the status of fallen creatures living on a minimal daily pittance. In 1925, the Czech composer Leoš Janáček composed an opera entitled *The Makropoulos Affair*, based on a play by Karel Čapek. The theme is the following: the singer Emilia Makropoulos, born in the sixteenth century, has served as a guinea pig for a magician who created an elixir of life. Still blooming, three centuries later, and still desirable, with a voice of an inalterable purity, Emilia is tired of not being able to grow old and die. She consumes the people around her by her longevity and abandon. She survives without attachment "in the middle of things and shadows," her children and her friends being without importance for her. "You're going to die, you others, you're lucky," she says to the normal people surrounding her. "Oh Lord, open the gates of night to me, so that I can go away and disappear."[11] Life without the horizon of death is nothing more than a long nightmare, and, of all the forms of boredom, that of the immortals seems the worst. They are doomed forever.

"Love what will never be seen twice"?[12]

During a conversation with a young poet, probably Rainer Maria Rilke, in a mountain setting, Sigmund Freud mentions the passing of the seasons. The poet feels no joy at the thought that all this beauty is doomed to be erased and that, in winter, it will be gone. These things that he wants to admire seem to him diminished by their provisional character. Freud replies that this fleetingness is precisely what makes them valuable, and that beauty and perfection are precious only because they do not last. If there existed a flower that flowered for only one night, the product of its blooming would not seem to us any the less sumptuous. Let us suppose, he wrote later, that a time comes when the paintings and statues we admire today have fallen apart or that after us comes a race of men who no longer understand the works of our poets and thinkers, or even a geological period in which everything that lives on earth will have become mute? Our enjoyment of these beautiful and perfect things would not be any less legitimate. The Ancients, including Marcus Aurelius, had already sensed this: the greatest civilizations will be submerged in oblivion, buried in dust. Everything will disappear, languages, species, empires. That is the price to be paid for having appeared one day in history.

Whereas Rilke expresses the melancholy of transitoriness, Freud exalts the joy of the perishable. To prolong their dialogue, let us imagine for a moment that Rilke's wish is granted: the beauties of nature would not pass away, nor would those of culture. Life would be a perpetual spring. Everything that has ever been built will be maintained. Forgetting, erasing and replacing would have become impossible, past centuries would remain present in an eternal retention. The constructions of all cultures of all times would pile up alongside one another. The sadness of the irrevocable would be succeeded by the despair of the interminable. We would be colonized and inhabited by all earlier civilizations and events experienced since our childhood. If everything didn't sink into oblivion one day, including ourselves, life would be intolerable; permanence would be as dreadful as being eclipsed. There is a poignant grandeur in what does not last, except in the blink of fleeting revelation, in the convergence of the instant and forever. This is well expressed in this poem by Jacques Prévert:

> Thousands and thousands of years
> Would not be enough
> To speak of
> The little second of eternity
> When you kissed me
> When I kissed you
> One morning in wintry light
> In Montsouris Park
> In Paris
> On the Earth
> The Earth that is a star.[13]

If there is a paradoxical sadness in ruins, that is because they embody, on the mineral scale, the petrification that lies in wait for us on the moral level, *the triumph of dead time over living time*. Every fervent European has been struck some time or another, in Rome, Prague, Venice, Vienna, Athens, Kraków or Granada, by the Stendhal syndrome: a feeling of suffocation in the presence of an excess of masterpieces. The hypertrophy of the world of yesterday, the great Greco-Roman, Arab-Andalusian and Austro-Hungarian mausoleums, all those stones in their splendor, the palaces, castles and basilicas, crush us. Not to mention the gigantic contemporary museums, where we suffer from a veritable surfeit of masterpieces. These baroque, gothic and romanesque marvels do not say to us: "Dare!" They transfix us as servants of the immemorial or as simple consumers of time past. Confronted by these sarcophagic constructions, we are seized by the contradictory desire both to preserve and to profane them. We are torn between the piety of preservation and the sacrilege of degradation. It is the task of education to wrench these dead stones away from archaeology alone in order to transform them into living edifices. It is a question of remaking the beating heart of our cities, of our nations, of integrating them into present times. Each generation has to respiritualize the great monuments if we don't want them to sink into mere commemoration or a kind of Panurge-like tourism. We will never finish reappropriating the past.

Such is the tragedy of human existence: we have to come to terms with what destroys us, admit regret and loss as consubstantial with the happiness of being. Melancholy about what passes may be nothing compared with the unhappiness of what would never disappear and would burden us with its presence in perpetuity.

> I just say to myself:
> "At this time, in this place,
> One day, I was loved, I loved ..."[14]

The martyrs of endurance

The utopia of a human who is augmented and not mortal is not new. Over the centuries, countless methods have been tried by the prophets of longevity: the injection of young blood, elixirs of life, restricted calorie intake, strict vegetarianism, magic serums, Bulgarian yoghurt, DHEA, etc.[15] In the absence of a miracle treatment that would guarantee each of us, through cell regeneration or cryogenization, a hundred years of life, there remains the other method: systematic privation. In the nineteenth century, August Comte already forced himself to abide by dreadful rules: limiting stimulants, tobacco, coffee, alcohol and nutrients, measuring out his food rations, and not indulging in sex, "the most disturbing of our instincts."[16] Alas, the founder of positivism was not to live past the age of fifty-nine, a meagre result for such an arduous effort. The main argument that can be given against militant supporters of immortality is that, by trying so hard not to die, they forget to live. Preserving cells and tissues, rebuilding defective parts like a mechanic, regular bio-testing, repro-gramming cells and intelligent implants risk absorbing all our energy and distracting us from the true question: what should we do with our free time? To try to prolong one's life by all means, foregoing alcohol, good food and love, reducing one's calorie intake, "eating less to live longer," and subjecting oneself to daily supplements of vitamins, cells and blood, like a methodical Dracula, is to forbid oneself to live in order to survive beyond a hundred years, at any price. Of course, longevity is the result of a genetic lottery and work on the self, but it sometimes reminds us of the chastisements of an ascetic in the Christian period. Let us acknowledge that we are all divided between the desire to take full advantage of our lives and the desire to spare ourselves in order to live longer. Some people want to hang on, while others want to feel, and most of us want to do both. The "hard desire to endure" (Paul Éluard: *le dur désir de durer*) becomes a canonical value, even if we have to conquer it at the price of terrible restrictions: like an American student, the hero of a report televised at the end of the twentieth century, who ate only one meal a day, consisting of cereal and natural juices, never drank a drop of alcohol, did not have sex and avoided masturbation – a highly dangerous activity – in order to reach the canonical age of 140. He admitted that, although he had a skeletal physique, he was terribly depressed. Such are the lives of the new martyrs of immortality. They obsess about the ways of prolonging life without wondering about the meaning of this prolongation, without seeing they are transforming their present into a hell. As Cicero put it, "even a short life is long enough to be beautiful and good."[17] People eagerly ask centenarians, both male and female, "What is your secret?" The answers invariably burst forth: laughing heartily, eating well, drinking well, loving abundantly, smoking cigars, not denying oneself anything. That's exactly what I do and I feel worse and worse. The medical school tells me to stop right away if I want to live out the year. But who are these people who allow themselves everything that is forbidden me? Where do they come from?

Gaining time: that used to mean keeping free moments when doing exhausting, servile work. Now it means a relentless productivism, a maniacal accumulation of days torn off the calendar. To want to remain forever is, in a way, to want to die on the job. Life is not, any more than love is, a marathon in which we have to go on as long as possible, by means of restrictions and check-ups; rather, it is a certain quality of relationships, emotions, commitments. When it is reduced to the simple rumination on our organs, an ongoing process of makeshift repairs, does it still have any value at all? What is sadder than those retirement homes where old people wait for the end, brooding over their memories, being fed, dressed, gotten out of bed, and washed like desiccated, babbling infants?

Whether one wants to abolish time, forget it or accelerate it, something has to happen in people's hearts that amounts to an upheaval, something unexpected. Intensity or prolongation: that is the choice to be made, which is obviously intolerable. *The dullness of long years without savor* vs. *the plenitude of a time truly lived.* The risk being that, instead of immortality, we end up with only a slipping away without grandeur. What mockery there is in this observation, drawn from the previously quoted novel by Italo Svevo: "Why do you keep smoking, despite the danger?" "Because I'm afraid I won't die." And let us recall Serge Gainsbourg, who smoked, for pleasure, right to the end, five packs a day (see https://en.wikipedia.org/wiki/Serge_Gainsbourg), despite four heart attacks (the fifth killed him in 1991).

The zombie in us

There are times when our lives atrophy and seem spiritually deactivated, like zombies in horror films, dead souls, puppets with neither brains nor passions, driven by an insatiable appetite for fresh flesh. These monsters, who appeared in Western painting as early as the Renaissance and whose name comes from Haiti, fascinate us: they embody a kind of grotesque immortality because they can neither live nor die, only devour everything that moves. What is a zombie? In film, a corpse that doesn't know it is still alive, and, in reality, a living being that doesn't know that it is already dead. It is a being that cannot speak: it can utter only a hoarse moan, an endless complaint that signals its doom as a damned creature. In the zombie, as it was established for us by George Romero's film,[18] stupor is mixed with ferociousness. It is a soul in pain that can remain prostrate for years on end and then suddenly awaken when living beings, animals or humans, approach or make noise. It eats, never sated, and eats messily, with gnawed fingers, letting intestines drip down its ravaged face like a vulture with no manners. A rotting creature that will never attain the calm of becoming a skeleton, it evokes a kind of morbid romanticism of putrefaction.

The equivalent of a zombie in our time are these neo-dead with an uncertain juridical status, preserved for the purposes of organ transplantation, legally cadavers, warm or cold, but still animated by a few vital functions.[19] The zombie is also an absent-minded being that has gotten the date wrong and returns too soon, parodying the resurrection promised at the end of time. It has to be killed again, if possible, by destroying its brain so that it will rest in peace and leave others alone. The Egyptian *Book of the Dead* maintains that you always die twice – first when the soul leaves your body and again when the last person who knew you dies. You don't disappear at the same rate from the memory of those who love you, and, if some people erase you quickly, despite their ostentatious sorrow on the day of your death, others continue to miss you. We do not die exactly on the day of our demise but, rather, before or after, when our descendants' mourning places us in the great chain of the dead. How many artists, singers, actors and politicians have died during their lifetimes, their names evoking for their contemporaries only a cruel: "I thought he died a long time ago!" Napoleon died on 5 May 1821, but it was almost two months before his death became known in England and France. The reactions were lukewarm: "It's no longer an event, it's a news item," Talleyrand pronounced. It is terrible to survive one's own career or reputation without being borne by it; whence some actors' admirable insistence on dying on stage, from the very thing that nourished them, transcended them.

We often behave, without realizing it, like cadavers endowed with speech but whose spring has broken, moved only by a mechanism without breath. A great challenge for all of us at every age: knowing how to rise up against the moral desert that is submerging us, how to ward off premature death. The hardest part is not to die someday, it's never to have succeeded in experiencing something essential in the realm of love or attachment. There comes a time when the onus of what we have been weighs on what we are. It is sometimes a considerable burden that we would like to be able put down, like a piece of baggage that is too heavy.

OLD INFANTS AND YOUNG DOTARDS

What is the baby-boomer generation? The one that exalted youth, theorized the rejection of authority, the end of hierarchies and of paternal power. Also the one that swept away every rule or taboo in the name of the omnipotence of desire, convinced that our passions, even the most unseemly, are innocent, and that multiplying them indefinitely is the way to come closest to bliss, great joy. But this indulgent generation wanted to teach its children nothing but the rejection of authority, which was identified with arbitrariness. It made its incompetence a dogma, its indifference a virtue, and its resignation the *nec plus ultra* of liberal pedagogy. The supremacy of fathers who were pals, of mothers who were girlfriends, denying all difference between them and their children and offering the latter only an ultra-permissive credo: do whatever you want. That is why these "adult juveniles" (Edgar Morin) did not equip their offspring for the tasks that awaited them and, believing that they were giving birth to a new humanity, raised anxious young people who are often tempted by conservatism. Hence, in their progeny, a demand for order, a moral rigidification and a need for points of reference at any cost: these young old people demand of their Peter Pan mothers and fathers that they finally acknowledge their age and their responsibilities. But pot-bellied, bald and myopic, the children of the baby boom, who have often become prominent and orderly, remain attached to their illusions. Old rascals to the end, alongside young worriers who are ageing prematurely, aware that their parents, by refusing to grow up, have stolen their youth.

Thus we see thirty-year-old post-adolescents lazing around their parents' home (also for economic reasons). Not to mention jihadists, who often come from families without a father and who offer their services to sanguinary satraps who, in the name of God, command them to take up arms, enslave women and kill, kill endlessly, to reach their paradise. A fine example of total anarchy that is inverted into supreme enslavement. (What is an anarchist? Someone who is nostalgic for absolute power and, because he has not found a despot who will break his neck, screams "Neither God nor master!") If every age group is based on the symbolic murder of the preceding one, the majority of today's boys and girls have been deprived of that advantage. That is the tragedy of excessively liberal educations founded on the absolute equality of generations. Transmission has been cut off the way a telephone line is cut.

A final example to date: the elevation of a young Swedish woman, Greta Thunberg, sixteen years old, into a heroine of the struggle against global warming. Nominated for the Nobel Prize, received by many heads of state and the pope. She carries in her wake tens of millions of high-school students, weeps for the planet and offers her anxious face, framed by two braids, as a symbol of the coming disaster. But our

Scandinavian Pythia, a cross between Fifi Brindacier and Joan of Arc, limits herself to repeating what the media have been drumming into us for years: namely, that the human adventure is over, that the apocalypse is near. A strange kind of ventriloquism: people are delighted to find in her and her followers the concerns that have been inculcated in them, and swoon over this infantile echolalia. The little parrots scold us by proxy, teach us a good lesson on which we are supposed to meditate. But it's a simple echo chamber, and we find among the puerile people the words that have been put in their mouths by continuous indoctrination. This nihilism with a childish face is directly inspired by catastrophist sects. The propaganda of fear is doing enormous damage among our children, whom we tell day and night that the globe will catch fire and cataclysms will destroy us. In the name of the just war against climate disturbance, we are creating terrified generations, and in so doing we are robbing them of their insouciance. We are paralyzing them more than we are mobilizing them. The right to conflate everyone's age makes it impossible for children to experience their childhood. The "Global Strike for the Future" is occurring just when we are explaining to young people that they don't have one, that the general collapse has begun. If concern about the environment is universal, the end-of-the-world disease is purely Western and says a great deal about our culture.

Our period gives priority to a single relation between ages: mutual pastiche. We ape our kids, who copy us. When adults dream of immaturity, the crushing burden of acting responsibly falls on their children. But this responsibility is dictated to them by professors of panic, who terrorize them instead of helping them confront the future. Indoctrination in despair ravages fragile, influenceable minds. It's no longer education; it's a curse, an evil spell that is cast on new generations on the verge of existence.

10

The Immortality of Mortals

There is only one advantage of falling ill when you're young, indeed, very young, and that is that you're less surprised later when, as age comes on, you have to take care of yourself and forego certain excesses. When death looms in childhood, it gives the days that follow a particular savor. You know the music, so to speak, the inexhaustible fertility of pain, hospital life, relapses and remissions. You've experienced vulnerability, and it doesn't feel like you're falling short when you have to take it easy. The sickly child often becomes a healthy adult. Remembering all the problems we have escaped helps us overcome later ones. And, like Odysseus, we say to ourselves: "Hold on, my heart, you have already survived crueller tests." We have come close to the worst, and above all we have known the joy of emerging from it: convalescence is a kind of negative happiness that consists primarily in the absence of unhappiness. A mad pleasure in recovering the use of one's limbs if one has been deprived of it, of rediscovering walking, appetite, the company of others. For someone who is leaving the hospital, the sanatorium or confinement in a sinister room, the very special moment comes when the ordinary becomes once again the extraordinary: the framework of the everyday, commonplace for everyone, has been transformed into a precious ideal. That happiness arises chiefly from the disappearance of unhappiness.

What do bodily ills teach us?

Illness teaches us at least three things: prudence, resistance and fragility. Blaise Pascal (1623–1662), in his *Prière à Dieu pour demander le bon usage des maladies* (Prayer to God to ask that illnesses be rightly used), saw illness as a divine punishment for a bad use of health, as a necessary correction, a way of detaching oneself from transient vanities, the deceptive pleasures of this world. In his view, it was a "scourge that consoles" and allows the sinner to get back on the path to God. The sufferer must look with favor on the wounds to his flesh, as Christ suffered to redeem humanity's sins. "And I ask, Lord, to feel all together both the pains of nature for my sins and the consolations of your Spirit by your grace." For Pascal, illness was a divine sign, a way of coming closer to the Creator through the pains endured. Thus God had to be thanked for inflicting this trial on you. In Pascal's prayer there is more than a morbid asceticism that revolts us: there is a pride in being elected through suffering, the certitude of being marked in one's body by the divine will.

Suffering is a message sent by God to his most faithful subjects, a language to be deciphered passionately, a particular gospel – almost a consolation. Then suffering is no longer suffering, it is rejoicing in having been designated by God as a creature worthy of interest. Pain is an advance on Purgatory, an essential stage on the road to Redemption.

177

It remains that an illness, no matter what it is, even a simple, miserable cold, is more than an accident. It is an adventure, another aspect of life of which everyone is both the victim and the beneficiary. Being at the mercy of one's bowels, bronchial tubes or joints is a fine lesson in humility. We "catch" a disease that arises in our innermost being and ends up dispossessing us of ourselves if it gets worse. Pain is a lesson in disillusionment if one overcomes it. It strikes us, awakens us, provides us with an identity, assigns us to an order: one is a cardiac patient, has a lung problem, suffers from arthritis, sclerosis or rheumatism, one has high blood pressure or high cholesterol, and one shares that condition with thousands of other people. We get together with people suffering from the same malady, we exchange anecdotes, advice, we feel less alone in our distress. That is why each society, each culture, has seized on our ailments to give them a different meaning. Any attack on health forces us to come up with a response: what demoralizes some people galvanizes others. Hence Romanticism raised each pathology to the rank of a prelude to inspiration: syphilis in Baudelaire and Maupassant, epilepsy in Dostoevsky, asthma in Proust, melancholy in Rousseau or Kafka, cancer in Fritz Zorn.

Tuberculosis has given rise to an impressive literature: in *The Magic Mountain*, didn't Thomas Mann describe the sanatorium at Davos, the Berghof, as a site for vacations and gaiety, whose atmosphere seduces the young Hans Castorp who has come, on the eve of World War I, to visit his cousin? Delighted by the place and people he meets, and having fallen in love with the young Clawdia Chauchat, he ends up remaining at high altitude, subjecting himself "to the principle of unreasonableness, to the brilliant principle of illness," sure that tuberculosis patients are the bearers of a special intelligence that the people of the lowlands do not have. And when, finally cured, he goes back down, it is to join in the belligerent madness of the Great War conceived by the masses, who are in theory "healthy." In other words, "to attain supreme health, one has first to traverse the profound experience of illness and death, just as the knowledge of sin is the first condition for redemption" (Thomas Mann). Healthy people are people who don't know they are sick, whereas patients are already awakened to a superior consciousness that makes their recovery unthinkable. The boundary between the normal and the pathological is blurred. Didn't the philosopher and theologian Franz von Baader (1765–1841) maintain, following the German theosophist and mystic Jakob Böhme (1575–1624), a cobbler by trade, that illness is the expression of a malfunctioning vitality, of a life-force that turns against itself and devours itself with its own energy?

Beyond these speculations, illness is not so much a disastrous or beneficial election as a statistical curse. It is inevitable that in the course of our lives we are all struck by it, with an increased risk after a certain age. No injustice, just a probability: *illness is the price of longevity.* Some illnesses protect you from more serious problems: they are firewalls whose recurrence might prevent you from being afflicted by other troubles. You don't really get over them; you learn to live with them, you contain them. Other illnesses are screens that lead diagnosis astray, hiding more serious changes that develop in the silence of your organs and secretly eat you away. We know the saying: if, after the age of fifty, you don't hurt somewhere, that's because you're dead. Pain is a certificate of vitality. It's the organism creaking, protesting and rebelling. In this respect, we are all "empirical physicians" for ourselves (Leibnitz), monitoring our bodies for signs of improvement or failing. Many people, despite their age, persist in feasting, drinking and living it up, paying no attention to the consequences. Others try to preserve their health, like old rockers who go directly from cocaine to green tea, from bourbon to mineral water. Some famous guitarists or singers, more wrinkled than a sequoia's bark, survivors of all kinds of orgies and overdoses, then seem to be endangered monuments that no subscription will ever be able to rehabilitate.

The hierarchy of pains

When we were young, the body was our friend, almost a servant. We didn't spare it: it had to be able to recover by itself, put itself back in order, and we were amazed by its reserves, its power. We felt invincible. After thirty, it rebels and ends up requiring constant attention. The servant becomes a demanding master who harasses us, and the line between casualness and concern becomes increasingly fine. Am I right to be alarmed or am I a coward? I've never been sick a day in my life, says the braggart. That's the time to start worrying. I've always been ill, and I've overcome every kind of miasma, says another. Be careful not to boast about it. The timorous see in the slightest malaise the symptom of an impending disaster. They have to see a doctor at once. Paleness, a palpitation, a dizzy spell when standing up, breathlessness, a lancing pain in the abdomen are all premonitory. And since society, in the name of prevention, is constantly warning us about all the possible pathologies, it creates whole generations of panicky people seeking treatment. Prudence becomes another name for terror. To which we have to add the category of the sick by hearsay: they contract all the diseases about which they are told, including those of their best friends. If that happens to other people, it has to happen to me, too ...

The Immortality of Mortals

Few people can live without a doctor: not that they are actually weakened, but they need someone to pay attention to them, to listen to them. Continual health – banal, monotonous, sempiternal – would be unbearable for them. Practicioners are obliged to attend to them, and the most admirable devotion is never enough. The ups and downs of the bruised body can give rise to subtle rivalries: how many people are proud of the ills that strike them and wave away anyone who has gone through lesser trials? "Your operation lasted only two and half hours? Rubbish! I was on the operating table for eight hours straight. I came out of a coma three times; I came close to dying." These are ostentatious patients. Their tribulations give them formidable stature, and they tell one terrifying anecdote after another, like soldiers telling stories about their experiences in combat. They belong to the aristocracy of distress and will not put up with being lumped in with small-time, two-bit malingerers. The body's ills have their quarters of nobility and their commoners. Plebeians stupidly endure the most dreadful failings, while nobles bear their torments with dignity, transform their infirmities into honorific medals. They have returned from the realm of limbo: they almost strip to exhibit their skin stitched with scars, sinister gashes that they display to intimidate you. They are proud of their stigmata; they are profane Christs crucified on the altar of Science. They forbid you to compare your tribulations with their trials. The ailment that afflicts them makes them garrulous; they feel obliged to communicate their story, right away. Each day is a new battle that they wage before witnesses; they offer a running account of their traumas and dominate the headlines. They don't want our compassion; they want to stagger us. The flipside of the bigmouth: the Stoic's discretion. The Stoic practices euphemism, laconically alluding to medical problems when he is on the brink of the grave.

As for the eagerness with which some people ask about your illness and offer to help you, it is suspect. They like you ill because they can't stand you when you're healthy; they feel less alone if they see you debilitated. Your suffering delights them; it makes their pain easier to bear. In the twenty-first century, to fall ill is both to be pleased with the unprecedented advances in medicine, with the leap forward that it will still make with artificial intelligence, immunotherapy, and to fear that it will not be able to save us. At a time when this discipline still was a kind of magic or sorcery, Montaigne protested against physicians who made "health sick" in order to exercise their authority and prescribed all sorts of unguents, ointments and diets in order to keep patients under their control. And he counted on customs and manners to keep himself healthy without consulting quacks. For our contemporaries, there is nothing more terrifying than reaching the limits of science. When a big shot, a top specialist, tells us he can do nothing further for us or for someone close to us, a bottomless pit opens before us. Modernity cannot tolerate failure; it sees it as laziness, ill will, the supreme obscenity. Like Montaigne, we know we're responsible for our own health. Independently of the hazards of our destiny or genetic capital, we are our own physicians, our own liberators or gravediggers. What is worse, for a superstitious person, than seeing his general practitioner die before he does? It's as if the order of priorities were inverted: the person who was supposed to take care of you failed to detect the disease that was going to kill him. What he said is virtually invalidated; he was supposed to remain at your bedside right to the end – he has betrayed you. Not to mention the professionals who set a bad example: the pulmonologist who smokes and coughs his lungs out, the obese dietician, the dermatologist with sunburn, the ear, nose and throat doctor who's deaf as a post. Although doctors see many of their patients waste away, there are patients who exhaust whole battalions of doctors, like the amorous man in his nineties in one of Gabriel García Márquez's novels who buries a whole family of physicians, one after the other, from the grandfather to the grandson, and outlives, hale and hearty, all their diagnoses.[1] In this respect, who is our favorite doctor? The one who tells us that we're fine, that it's a false alarm. We come out of his office, relieved, until a little voice perfidiously suggests that he might have been mistaken: it would be wiser to seek a second opinion to confirm the first one. For the tormented patient, anxiety is endless: it makes his life dramatic and becomes indispensable for providing it with variety and interest.

In the end, there is an undeniable pleasure in getting over an infection, the joy, Spinoza would say, of knowing that a hateful thing has been destroyed, of talking about a danger that we know we have escaped. There is nothing we admire more than someone who has survived an accident, an avalanche, an earthquake, or a handicapped person who begins to walk again, a dying patient who emerges from a coma – examples that challenge science, especially when it has declared that they were doomed. It is the survivors who help us put up with our condition, brighten our darkest moods by offering us an unjustified hope. A marvellous feeling of having come close to the abyss without having fallen into it. Recovering the use of our limbs, of our bodies, of our strengths, rising from our bed of pain, escaping the humiliating dependency on others, is a delicious moment that plunges us back into everyday well-being. We return, astonished to still be alive, and we say to ourselves: I'm stronger than I thought I was. If I can cope with that I'll be able to wage other wars, mobilize new resources. *The only meaning of illness is to fight it*, even if over time it becomes a double interwoven with our

183

lives. We keep it at a distance, although we sense that the battle is endless. Pain teaches us nothing, in no way makes us better. We take care of ourselves, not in the hope of recovering but only with the wish to adjourn disaster. The spectre of the end makes each day's light more luminous.

There is, in this respect, *a tragic optimism* that arises from our dialogue with life when, at the end of a long struggle, it returns to us the confidence that we give it. We confront scourges resolutely and humbly, determined not to kneel down before them. The contemporary citizen is a suffering subject in revolt against his suffering. His fragility is also his asset in a community of fertile concern that connects him with other patients. What distinguishes people at every age is the energy that they deploy and that supports them. This person seems to be an oak brought down by a trifle, while another who had already been buried survives all agonies and persists in being, still fully alive.

Poor consolations

In the eighth book of his *Mémoires d'outre-tombe*, Chateaubriand tells how, on returning from North America in 1792, he barely survived a storm at sea between England and France. "I was not disturbed during this near shipwreck and felt no joy in being saved. Better to escape from life when one is young than to be driven out of it by time."[2] That is truly the view of a braggart who is certain that he has an eternity before him. Disgust with existence at the age of twenty seems a spoiled child's luxury. How much more profound is this remark by Jean Paulhan – "I hope to live until I die" – which recalls a joke told by dissidents in the Soviet bloc: "The Party tells us that there is no life after death, that religion is the opium of the people. But is there a life before death?" Let us note in this regard that the jihadists, for their part, do not believe in life before death: they are biophobes. Life, as it really is, unpredictable, unexpected, terrifies them. They want to get out of it, as soon as possible, by killing a maximum of innocent people and presenting a marvellous harvest of corpses to their sanguinary God. They blow themselves up in order to be spared uncertainty – that is, freedom.

Confronted by the scandal of death, philosophy, which is as rich in tranquilizers as religions are, has invented all kinds of subterfuges, including the ancient genre of "Consolations," which has given rise to genuine master-pieces.[3] What is this all about? Confronting adversity in advance the better to disarm it when it strikes. Putting before one's eyes, as a spiritual propaedeutic exercise, *praemedito*, all the possible sources of suffering and diffi-culty, so as not to be surprised when they occur.[4] We have to use imaginary misfortune to prepare ourselves for real misfortune and rid ourselves of the fear of death, of illness, of misery, by simulating them, the better to deprive them of their power. For example, we can sleep without shelter, live on brown bread and water, wear crude garments, and engage in sessions of fictitious poverty to avoid fearing the loss of wealth. "Accustom yourself to everything that discourages you."[5] We have to imagine the worst in order to accept it without flinching when it happens. Seneca cites the case of a Roman general, Pacuvius, the conqueror of Syria, who had himself buried every evening after funereal drinking and feasting, as if he were going to die the same night. He imitated death, applauded by his guests, and this pantomime was for him a pretext for perpetual debauchery. "Let us, however, do from a good motive what he used to do from a debased motive; let us go to our sleep with joy and gladness; let us say: I have lived; the course which Fortune set for me is finished. And if God is pleased to add another day, we should welcome it with glad hearts."[6]

Let us admit that such a viaticum is likely to produce severe insomnia. We anticipate possible distresses to avoid being taken by surprise if they befall us. No matter how prudent we are, we are always surprised by the illness that strikes us, by the setbacks we suffer and by death, which we know is inevitable. Stoicism is a voluntarist fatalism: we have to welcome with joy, as in conformity with the order of the world, the most painful trials. "Seek not that the things which happen should happen as you wish; but wish the things which happen to be as they are, and you will have a tranquil flow of life."[7] The worst-case scenario, maintained by great tormented persons, is still a kind of conjuring: believing that the abominable will not happen because we have imagined it. Preventive anxiety is a perverse form of optimism. During the great debate that took place in France in 2019, activists proposed that elected officials complete training programs in obligatory poverty to make them sensitive to the condition of excluded people. But a brief experience of being stone broke, far from waking us up, may make affluence even more desirable and poverty more detestable. As for the exercises in pain or simulated privation advocated by the Ancients, they in no way help us endure real misfortunes when they happen to us. Foreseeing in detail the harm that will befall us has never protected us against it. The affliction is not attenuated by anticipating it. When it happens, we are upset, scandalized.

The certainty of dying one day transforms life into a tragedy and a passion: the transitory nature of all things increases our will to seize life by the horns. As soon as a child is born, he is old enough to die, says a German proverb; but, conversely, replies modernity, we are always too young to die, because science and medicine have pushed back the frontiers of the end and we are indignant to have to leave at any age. As early as 1886, Leo Tolstoy remarked, in a short novel entitled *The Death of Ivan Ilyich*, the extent to which death had become, for the society of his time, a nauseating annoyance, not without indecency.[8] Sigmund Freud, in turn, noted in 1915, in the middle of World War I, that societies no longer accept the natural character of death and reduce it to the rank of a fortuitous accident due to illness, to infection. Dying ceased to be normal some time ago.[9] It could have been otherwise, we could have nibbled another year or two, and that's what's unbearable. The physical and mental incapacity of the old person vegetating in a hospice for years is worse than death. Incapacitating illness, the kind that strikes you off the rolls of humanity and transforms you into a drooling, spitting vegetable, is more atrocious than dying. That is what rightly terrifies us. Classical anxiety confronted imperfect believers with the perspective of eternal punishment in the flames of Hell. The modern nightmare is an interminable survival on a hospital bed, with all faculties diminished, at the mercy of others.

Just a moment, Mr Executioner

Death is not an evil, St Augustine wrote, when it follows a good life; it opens the way to the gates of Paradise – that is, to deliverance from sin.[10] But that is an argument that does not convince the non-believer, and it in no way attenuates the shock of the end. Isn't it the inverse that occurs? When life has become, as it has for us, the supreme value, to which all others are subordinated, death and pain seem intolerable. Is it so true that we die better when we have lived well, "full of days"? Who decides that we have lived well and that that suffices? Another moral tonic: to overcome death, we have to maintain otherness (Emmanuel Levinas). It's a fine formula, but it's particularly ineffective when it's people we love – that is, otherness par excellence – who die. Or again: "What does dying matter, since we have avoided the death that consists in missing out on life!"[11] It is terrible, of course, to miss out on the essential, but the feeling that one has had a full life does not make the end less atrocious. Even an earth-bound destiny is reluctant to disappear. According to some writers, death is not an event in life. Epicurus: "Death, therefore, the most awful of evils, is nothing to us, seeing that, when we are, death is not come, and, when death is come, we are not.."[12] In a sublime sermon, Bossuet retorted that death is in the very air we breathe, the food we eat, "even the remedies with which we try to defend ourselves against it," because it resides in the source of life itself.[13]

The fact is that death comes whether we want it to or not, and no philosophy or religion, however generous it might be, can mask its horror. We leave the scene one day, and the banquet goes on without us. "On the threshold of the Great Night that is so dark, the wise man is only a poor orphan" (Vladimir Jankélévitch). All those lofty sophisms are in danger of being swept away when the time comes, and the person who is going to die pleads to be granted a reprieve. Then every minute weighs a century, every second is as trenchant as a guillotine's blade. Just another moment, please, Mr Executioner. Under those circumstances, who does not, in spite of himself, *beg for prolongation*? "A day will come when a quarter of an hour will seem to us more valuable and more desirable than all the fortunes in the Universe" (Fénelon).[14]

Eternity is here and now

By permitting the birth of new generations, death is the guardian of beginnings and the preserver of diversity. The consequence of the grace of birth is the fatality of death, which authorizes its blooming. "Children's birth is the parents' death," said Hegel in a striking formula. What in us does not die? First of all, our progeny, as Plato already pointed out in the *Symposium* through the voice of Diotima, since procreation, by substituting a young individual for an older one, guarantees the perpetuity of the species choosing to maintain itself. Having children, in reasonable numbers, is a way of showing an *a priori* love of life in its endless flowering. And the propaganda of fanatical ecologists which opposes new births in the name of the "planet" is nothing less than a criminal nihilism that seeks to extinguish any human presence. Life is in love with itself; it is its own raison d'être and rejoices in its proliferation in the person of the children, both boys and girls, who renew it. Now the beyond, even for believers, is first of all our descendants. Everything that expands us is also immortal: the friendships formed, the romances experienced, the shared passions, the commitments made to others, the good deeds done.

A life is worthy of being lived only if it includes greater domains and intersects with *these relative absolutes* we call love, truth and justice. Glory is not reserved for a small number of heroes or saintliness for a few righteous persons; on the other hand, the humblest life inevitably encounters beauty, brotherhood, kindness. Our essence is to satisfy our ambitions, but it is also to live above ourselves, to participate in broader adventures, to feel at least once the sense of the infinite. Each of us is simultaneously a point and a bridge, a closed totality and a site of transition. This incomplete totality will someday disappear, will no longer be anything but a mark on a register, an algorithm on a screen, an inscription on a tomb. It sometimes happens that a heroic death – that of Seneca, for example, who committed suicide at the command of Nero, whose tutor he had been, by opening his veins – redeems a career of toadying and compromising with power.[15] In this regard, let us note, like Michel Serres, that the contemporary hero has more to lose than the classical hero, who was in any case doomed to die between twenty-five and thirty years later. The former's sacrifice is all the more sublime because he is risking a potentially considerable existential heritage.

Rather than seeking an improbable paradise, why not see immortality as the ability to reincarnate ourselves multiple times in this life? "There is something in us that does not die," said Bossuet, "a divine brightness," a door that opens on deliverance. According to him, on the threshold of death, the soul should rejoice to finally be moving toward its truth. For the agnostic, this admirable flame that keeps us going is the certainty that the Redemption will not occur at the end of life but, rather, is present, here and now. Eternity is what we are living in this precise moment. There is no other.

My death is, to be sure, terrible, but much less than the death of people I love, without whom I would not want to be alone in this world. My death is a horrible formality; the death of the people I love is an ontological catastrophe. The gradual extinction of persons dear to us as we grow older depopulates the world and makes the survivor an anachronism in an empty universe. "Living a long time means surviving many persons," said Goethe. So all that we are allowed is *a brief eternity*. As long as we love, as long as we create, we remain immortal. We have to cherish life enough to accept that one day it will leave us and hand over its enjoyment to the following generations.

190

THE DELICATE ART OF CONSOLATION

The comfort given those who are suffering is threatened by two abysses: formalism and mad syllogism. Roman philosophy is full of arguments as noble as they are pathetic – for example, encouraging a victim to resign himself to his misfortune by considering the fact that it could have been worse. You've lost a hand? Take consolation in the thought that you could have lost your whole arm. Your eye is infected and is about to fall out? Rejoice that the other one is still intact. We have to transform the loss into a gain, imagine what is worse in order to see ourselves as lucky. (But isn't that what we do spontaneously when we emerge unhurt from an accident, for example, with at most a few scratches?) Comforting a mother, Marcia, who had seen her son die, Seneca told her that she had to consider herself fortunate to have seen him live such a long time on the path of virtue. Had he grown old, he might have fallen into debauchery, been imprisoned, exiled or forced to commit suicide.[16] Ultimately, since "Not to be born, therefore, is the happiest lot of all,"[17] the lost son had to rejoice that he had returned at a very young age to his initial state before birth. "Blush, then, to do any mean or common action, or to weep for those dear to you who have been changed for the better."[18]

This refutation of suffering can go as far as insensitivity: if for us the worst of sorrows is the loss of the beloved person, reacting to it as Epictetus did – "Never say about anything: I have lost it. Rather: I have given it back. Your wife has died, she has been given back. Your child has died, he has been given back" – requires extraordinary violence except for someone who has raised *ataraxia* to the rank of a virtue. One might as well prefer officials of fictitious sorrow such as the employees of a funeral home, who barely manage to look compassionate. At least we don't expect from them anything but a service. An unhappy love affair, a break-up, financial ruin, a death or an illness require different words and counsels. Some people engage in concrete actions, others in a longer period of introspection. After the death of his beloved daughter Tullia, Cicero, devastated, turned toward study, read at the home of his friend Atticus all the texts "by anyone at all, on the alleviation of sorrow," and finally wrote a *Consolatio*, a sort of self-therapy in which he exhorts himself to master his sadness.

And yet, as soon as we are confronted with the sorrow of someone dear to us, or with mourning, we fall back, in spite of ourselves, on the rather soppy, sentimental sermons that we blame in rabbis, priests, imams and moralists during funerals. "God gave her to us, God has taken her back." Religions continue to be incomparable systems for transfiguring suffering and death. Through them a collectivity finds a meaning in the death of its members and makes it tolerable to the survivors. To comfort a friend or relative is to encourage them to bow before a power stronger than they are. This exceptional misfortune needs to be, over time, transformed into an ordinary misfortune and be seen as one of the necessities of nature. "What can happen to one individual can happen to anyone" (Publilius Syrus). We immerse a particular case in the generality of the human condition. The person who consoles must put himself in the place of his friend or relative and make the latter accept the ineluctable.

He would expect no less from others if he were struck by misfortune in turn. The convention is horrible but irrefutable. In many societies, mourning is limited by official regulation. The goal is to put an end to sterile pain by means of a collective medication. The heart must be reconciled with the social order that gradually smothers personal regrets. It is the irrefutable selfishness of the living who take back their rights over the dead. To help people, it often suffices to listen, to let their sorrow be freely expressed. The supreme form of delicacy in the matter of consolation is to be there and to surround the person with a vast ring of affection until she can fly again on her own wings.

Love, Celebrate, Serve

A 46-year-old man, accompanied by a pretty girl, stops his car near a tobacconist's shop that is still open at two o'clock in the morning. When he gets out of the car, ferocious cries ring out and a group of young people attack him. His offense? He has lived to be over forty, he's an insult to humanity. Age is a crime, that is the slogan of these nocturnal vigilantes. Their targets are mainly old fogeys consorting with women less than thirty; the sight of these ill-assorted couples makes their blood boil. The man signals to his companion to flee and he begins to run, pursued by seven or eight husky brutes. Their leader, Regora, wants to settle a personal beef with him. The quadragenarian, who is in good physical shape, succeeds in keeping ahead of them for part of the night. If he can keep it up until dawn, he's saved; the police will protect him. However, Regora catches up with him at the last minute and throws him into a ditch. The hunt is over. But it has exhausted the lyncher. And when the sun rises he has become an old man, whose hair has turned white in a single night and whose teeth have fallen out. His troops turn against him and prepare to put him to death.

A marvellous fable by Dino Buzzati. A day comes when the rising generations look on us as we used to look on our elders: with disdain and commiseration. It's a terrible life lesson, the return of the boomerang: we have become the people we scorned, years ago.

To understand the world and act on it, we have endlessly to interweave the generations with ties of friendship, common interests and conversation to promote as much exchange as possible. Each generation has a spiritual mentality marked by precise historical events, almost a full-fledged society that emerges from its blinders only when it is connected to the preceding and following generations. After the age of fifty, all of us, male or female, poor or rich, feel ourselves gradually slipping, at varying rates of speed, toward the world of yesterday. Whatever our efforts, we fear that we are losing our footing. If to grow up involves self-affirmation, growing old involves tottering. Having lived means not that I am a possessor but that I have been dispossessed. I have been deprived of all those past years that add up negatively, as it were, by subtracting themselves from my being. I can't accumulate them as assets; on the contrary, they appear as debits on my balance sheet. Time steals my certainties, diminishes my resolution.

If childhood is by nature ungrateful, that is because it needs all its strength to construct itself; gratitude comes later, when we feel capable of being disinterested and making sacrifices. Life is simultaneously a gift and a debt: an absurd gift given us by Providence and a debt that we have to repay to those close to us. There comes a time when we have to return to our family, our friends, our parents, our homeland, the benefits they have lavished on us. We don't repay our life debts; we recognize them, and honor them by taking care of our descendants in turn. The day when the debt is extinguished is also the day when life is extinguished, when we can no longer give or return anything to others, and we become, through death, the prey of the living.

We have predecessors just as we will have successors; we are mere temporary residents in a life that was not given to us, but lent. We have the use of it, but it is not our property. Growing old does not diminish our duties, as people think; on the contrary, it multiplies them. To live longer we have to begin by taking on new obligations. Freedom is not a relaxation but an increase of responsibilities. It does not lighten our burden but makes it heavier. Old people have a right to respect and repose, said Charles Péguy in 1912. Maybe they did, in his time. But these days! Life is not an illness from which we have to recover. At any age, salvation resides in work, commitment, study.

Each destiny is a bridge built between two chasms. We are not indispensable for anyone; we will disappear in the cosmos, anonymous dust, but that is no reason for sadness. On the contrary: life, as we have said, always has the structure of a promise. A promise of what? That is not specified. No fairy has leaned over our cradle. The only promise kept and that can never be erased is what we have experienced. That alone should elicit in us an infinite gratitude.

Right to the end, we must remain beings that say yes, that adhere unconditionally to what is: we must celebrate the splendor of the world, its dazzling wonders. Living on this earth is a miracle, even if it is an endangered miracle. To mature is to enter into an endless exercise of admiration, to find countless occasions to marvel at the grace of an animal, of a landscape, of a work of art, of a piece of music. The better to combat the disfiguration of the world, we must also bow before its sublimities, rediscover the necessary enchantments. If some people have lost their illusions as they grew older, that is because these illusions did not deserve to continue to live; they were mere adolescent fancies or congenial utopias. Better to adhere passionately to passing time than to curse it.

So we have to live beyond our physical, intellectual and amorous means, as if we had just inherited an immense fortune, as if we had at our disposal, even at the age of seventy or eighty, an allotment of additional years, a golden age. Ever since childhood, we have learned only one thing: the priceless value of life. We remain transitory beings, lost on a dark path and trying to find our way by the light of reason and beauty. We remain free only by immersing ourselves among others – brothers, friends, companions, parents – always curious, never resigned. We will lose our corporal envelope, disappear in the flux, become ashes once again. So what? We have always been transitory, part of a whole that transcends us. Let us rejoice to have continued to live and still to be able to enjoy the bounties of this world.

In the evening of life, however happy or painful it may be, we gauge the good fortune we've been given. We have been simultaneously hurt and fulfilled. Many of our prayers have not been heard; others, which we haven't formulated, have been granted a hundred times over. We have gone through nightmares and received treasures. Life has been cruel as well as heady and opulent.

The only word we ought to utter every morning, in recognition of the gift we have been given, is: Thanks.

We were owed nothing.

Thanks for this mad grace.

Notes

Introduction

1 Michel Philibert, *L'Échelle des âges* (Paris: Seuil, 1968), p. 63.
2 Here I refer the reader to the first part of *The Temptation of Innocence* (New York: Algora, 2000), where I analyze the metamorphoses of old age and the West's overestimation of childhood and immaturity.

Chapter 1 Giving Up on Giving Up

1 Patrice Bourdelais, in *Le Débat*, no. 82 (1994), points out that, in 1750, only 7 to 8 percent of the French population celebrated their sixtieth birthday. In 1985, 82 percent of adults and up to 92 percent of women reached the age of sixty. Today, a sexagenarian often still has their parents and relatives, including siblings, children and grandchildren. As many as four generations may live together in a single family, especially in the case of women. In the eighteenth century, old age began when one could no longer bear arms – that is, at sixty. Although the maximum life expectancy hardly extends beyond 110 years, more and more people

are living that long. In France, the number of people over a hundred years old is increasing by 7 percent a year.

2 The Romans distinguished, for men only, seven ages: *infans*, from 0 to 6, *puer* from 7 to 16, *adulescens* from 17 to 29, *juvenis* from 30 to 45, *senior* from 46 to 59, *senex* from 60 to 79, and *aetate provectus*, beyond 80, "advanced in age" or, word for word, "by the time of life pushed forward." Latin has two words for time: *tempus* and *aetas*. *Aetas* is the time of life, derived from the word *aevum*, which means life and length of life – in Greek, *aïon*, which also referred to the spinal cord, considered the seat of life.

3 In Japan, 40 percent of the population will be more than 65 years old in 2040. Today, there are 65,000 Japanese centenarians. In China, where the single-child policy did not make it possible to ensure the renewal of generations, there are only 22.6 million citizens over 80. The decline in the birth-rate threatens to slow the development of the country, which will be old before it is rich, according to the official formula. In India, 87 million persons are over 60, half of whom are poor and without income. In 2060, there will be 200,000 centenarians in France. Since 2014, life expectancy has leveled out in France, at 79.4 for men and 85.3 for women. The phenomenon affects all developed countries, though experts are unable to identify an unequivocal cause. France nonetheless remains one of the world leaders in matters of life expectancy. On this subject, see Jean-Hervé Lorenzi, François-Xavier Albouy and Alain Villemeur, *L'Erreur de Faust: essai sur la société du vieillissement* (Paris: Descartes, 2019).

4 According to Angus Deaton, who won the Nobel Prize in economics, the life expectancy in the Appalachians is lower than that in Bangladesh. He explains this epidemic of death by social despair, obesity and the opioid crisis, a massive consumption of painkillers sold by unscrupulous pharmaceutical companies that causes a staggering number of overdoses. This mortality rate also affects the white working classes in Great Britain, and it would be interesting to see if

the "Yellow vest" movement in France arises from the same problems. Let us remember that, in France, the difference in life expectancy between the richest 5 percent and the poorest 5 percent is thirteen years.

5 On this subject, see the very personal and literary book by Christine Jordis, *Automnes: plus je vieillis, plus je me sens prête à vivre* (Paris: Albin Michel, 2017).

6 Quoted by Georges Poulet, *Studies on Human Time*, trans. Elliott Coleman (New York: Harper Torchbooks, 1959), p. 58.

7 Martin Heidegger, *What is Metaphysics?*, Questions I and II.

8 Jean-Paul Sartre, *Les Mots* (Paris: Gallimard, 2011), pp. 201–2.

9 On this redefinition of the ages of life, see the foundational book by Michel Philibert, *L'Échelle des âges* (Paris: Seuil, 1968). See also Marcel Gauchet, "La Rédefinition des âges de la vie," *Le Débat*, no. 132 (2004–5), pp. 27–44, and the magisterial synthesis by Éric Deschavanne and Pierre-Henri Tavoillot, *Philosophie des âges de la vie* (Paris: Grasset, 2007).

10 Søren Kierkegaard, *Stages on Life's Way*, trans. Howard V. Hong and Edna H. Hong (Princeton NJ: Princeton University Press, [1845] 1991).

11 See Laurent Schwartz, *Vers la fin des maladies? Une approche révolutionnaire de la médecine* (Paris: Les liens qui libèrent, 2019). In his preface, Joël de Rosnay credits Dr Schwartz with replacing complexity by a "simplexity" that would allow us to group illnesses together in a few large categories to treat them in an overall way. If he succeeded in doing so, that would be a major advance for tomorrow's personalized, predictive and proactive medicine.

12 According to the biologist Jean-François Bouvet, we are living longer, but longer in poor health. For life expectancy to increase, the battle against cancer and neuro-degenerative diseases would have to make progress for both men and women. On the other hand, if for a centenarian the probability of dying within a year is 50 percent, that probability decreases after the age of 105, according to Elisabetta Barbi

of Sapienza University in Rome (a study that appeared in the journal *Science* on 29 June 2018). To be sure, the news is encouraging, but we would still have to get there, to be among the "happy few."

13 Anne-Laure Boch, neurobiologist, in *Le Débat*, no. 174 (2013).
14 *Le Figaro Magazine*, 14 November 1992.
15 In France, in the 1990s, a program called "Chronos" led by the Jean-Dausset Foundation took blood samples from nonagenarians and from the supercentenarian Jeanne Calment (whose record longevity was questioned in 2018 by Russian scientists). On epigenetics, see Joël de Rosnay, *La Symphonie du vivant* (Paris: Editions LLL, 2018).
16 David Le Breton, *L'Adieu au corps* (Paris: Métaillé, 2013), p. 13.
17 On the progress of the technosciences and the uberization of society, see Luc Ferry, *La Révolution transhumaniste* (Paris: Plon, 2016).
18 Gaston Bachelard, *La Psychanalyse du feu* (Paris: Gallimard, 1992), p. 39.
19 Philibert, *L'Échelle des âges*, p. 199.
20 Vladimir Jankélévitch, *L'Austérité* (Paris: Flammarion, 1956), p. 38, quoted in Lucien Jerphagnon, *Connais-toi toi-même ... et fais ce que tu aimes* (Paris: Albin Michel, 2012), p. 296.
21 Some jurists suggest establishing a senior system to protect weakened people from swindlers and to promulgate a "simple presumption of vulnerability" different from guardianship. This measure would be reversible in the event of a psychological or physical improvement of the person to be protected. Didier Guével, professor of private law, in *Recueil Dalloz*, no. 22 (2018).
22 See J. B. Pontalis, *Ce temps qui ne passe pas* (Paris: Gallimard, 1997).

Chapter 2 Staying in the Dynamics of Desire

1 In Russia, Vladimir Putin's decision in 2018 to postpone the age of retirement to sixty-five, whereas life expectancy, because of alcoholism and deficient medical care, is 67.5 for men, was very badly received. In Belgium, retirement will be set at sixty-seven in 2020, as it already is in Germany. France has set retirement at sixty-two under certain conditions, while, to balance the budget, recommending that it be delayed until sixty-four. What must be avoided at all costs is a covert battle between generations, because the young will have to pay for the old, who, moreover, are leaving them an enormous deficit: "Gains in longevity have to be considered as idle life at the expense of the working generations. A monstrosity in conflict with the obvious facts" – François de Closets, quoted in Colette Mesnage, *Éloge d'une vieillesse heureuse* (Paris: Albin Michel, 2013), p. 190.
2 See Jean Starobinsky, "L'Ordre du jour," in *Le Temps de la réflexion* (Paris: Gallimard, 1983), pp. 123–4.
3 Quoted by Norberto Bobbio, *Le Sage et la politique*, trans. Pierre-Emmanuel Dauzat (Paris: Albin Michel, 2004), p. 101.
4 Eric Deschavanne and Pierre-Henri Tavoillot, *Philosophie des âges de la vie* (Paris: Grasset, 2007), pp. 494ff.
5 "Age and happiness," *The Economist*, 18 December 2010.
6 "We rediscover at 70 the happiness of a young person of 30. At 80, we have found (on average) the joy of being 18. How can we understand this surprising result? Old age frees us of a burden, that of accumulating useless goods, and restores intrinsic goods to their place," writes Daniel Cohen, commenting approvingly on a poll in his *Homo economicus: prophète égaré des temps nouveaux* (Paris: Albin Michel, 2013), p. 27.
7 See Deschavanne and Tavoillot, *Philosophie des âges de la vie*, p. 487.
8 In France, the law allows one to supplement a pension by

parallel work, with different modalities for government employees and liberal professions. For the moment, only a tiny percentage of retirees, 5 percent, take advantage of this.

9 Louis Aragon, "Il n'y a pas d'amour heureux," in *La Diane française* (Paris: Seghers, 1946).
10 Seneca, *Letters to Lucilius*, 24.
11 François Rivière, *J.-M. Barrie: le garçon qui ne voulait pas grandir* (Paris: Calmann-Lévy, 2005), and Béatrice Balti, *J.-M. Barrie: celui qui préférait les fées aux femmes* (Paris: Éditions Complicités, 2018).

Chapter 3 The Saving Routine

1 Italo Svevo, *Zeno's Conscience*, trans. William Weaver (New York: Vintage, 2003), p. 12.
2 Ibid., p. 29.
3 Louis Jerphagnon, *Connais-toi toi-même … et fais ce que tu aimes* (Paris: Albin Michel, 2012), p. 236.
4 Michel de Montaigne, *Complete Essays of Montaigne*, trans. Donald M. Frame (Stanford, CA: Stanford University Press, 1958), bk II, chap. 37, p. 575.
5 With Bill Murray and Andie MacDowell, directed by Harold Ramis, 1993.
6 Reported by Michel Tournier, "Cinq clefs pour André Gide," in *Le Vol du vampire* (Paris: Gallimard, 1983), pp. 224–5.
7 Thomas Mann, *The Magic Mountain* (New York: Vintage, 1996), pp. 180–1.
8 Montaigne, *Complete Essays*, bk. 3, chap. 2, p. 620.
9 Søren Kierkegaard, *Fear and Trembling* and *Repetition*, trans. Howard V. Hong and Edna H. Hong (Princeton, NJ: Princeton University Press, 1983), pp. 131ff.
10 Quoted in Lisa Halliday, *Asymmetry* (New York: Simon & Schuster, 2018).
11 Plato, *Timaeus*, trans. Benjamin Jowett (Oxford: Oxford University Press, 2019), 37d.

12 Daniel Mendelsohn, *An Odyssey: A Father, a Son, and an Epic* (New York: Vintage, 2019), p. 16.

13 Jorge Luis Borges, "Pierre Ménard, Author of the *Quixote*," trans. James E. Irby, in Borges, *Labyrinths* (New York: New Directions, 1964), pp. 36–44.

14 A play on a line from Mallarmé's poem "Brise marine": "La chair est triste, hélas, et j'ai lu tous les livres" [Trans.].

15 Henry David Thoreau, *Walden* (New York: Modern Library, 1992), p. 32.

16 Quoted in Michel Philibert, *L'Échelle des âges* (Paris: Seuil, 1968), p. 102.

17 Gilles Deleuze distinguished American lines of flight, which are a way of resuming an interrupted line by adding to it a zig-zag segment, whereas the French, following in the footsteps of Descartes or the French Revolution, seek an absolute point of departure and rupture. "It is never the beginning or the end that are interesting; the beginning and the end are points. What is interesting is the middle. The English zero is always in the middle." Gilles Deleuze and Claire Parnet, *Dialogues* (Paris: Champs Flammarion, 2008), p. 50.

18 Charles Baudelaire, *Curiosités esthétiques*, quoted in Philibert, *L'Échelle des âges*, p. 103.

19 Friedrich Nietzsche, *Beyond Good and Evil*, §245, trans. Helen Zimmern, www.gutenberg.org/files/4363/4363-h/4363-h.htm.

20 David Riesman, *Individualism Reconsidered*, 1954, quoted in Philibert, *L'Échelle des âges*, pp. 214–15.

21 On this subject, see Michel Tournier, "Émile Ajar ou la vie derrière soi," in *Le Vol du vampire*, pp. 340ff.

22 Julien Gracq, *En lisant, en écrivant* (Paris: José Corti, 1981).

23 "Les formes cycliques de Wolfgang Rihm," *Le Monde*, 12 February 2019.

24 Karl Marx, *The Eighteenth Brumaire of Louis Bonaparte* (Moscow: Progress, 1937), §1, www.marxists.org/archive/marx/works/1852/18th-brumaire/.

25 Jean-Paul Sartre, *Situations* I (Paris: Gallimard, 2010), p. 365.

Chapter 4 The Interweaving of Time

1 Henry James, *The Altar of the Dead* (London: Martin Secker, 1916), chap. 3, www.gutenberg.org/files/642/642-h/642-h.htm.
2 Aristotle, *Nicomachean Ethics*, Book 10, chap. 7, "On pleasure and true happiness," 1178a.
3 Seneca, *Letters to Lucilius*, no. 61.
4 "Remember that you are going to die."
5 "The human plagiarism which it is most difficult to avoid, for individuals (and even for nations which persevere in their faults and continue to aggravate them) is the plagiarism of ourselves." *The Remembrance of Things Past*, trans. C. K. Scott-Moncrieff, vol. 6, *The Sweet Cheat Gone* (London: Chatto & Windus, 1969).
6 Victor Hugo, *How to Be a Grandfather*, trans. Timothy Adès (London: Hearing Eye, [1877] 2012).
7 François Mauriac, *Le Noeud de vipères* (Paris: Livre de Poche, 1973), p. 177.
8 Hannah Arendt, *La Crise de la culture* (Paris: Gallimard, 1972), p. 247.
9 Gaston Bachelard, *La Poétique de la rêverie* (Paris: PUF, 1968), p. 114.
10 Ibid.
11 Serge Tisseron, *Les Secrets de famille* (Paris: PUF, 2011), pp. 83–4.
12 Germaine Dieterlen, *Essai sur la religion bambara* (Paris: PUF, 1951), quoted in Michel Philibert, *L'Échelle des âges* (Paris: Seuil, 1968), p. 84.
13 Matthieu Galey, *Journal, 1974–1986* (Paris: Grasset, 1989).
14 Plato, *Symposium*, 219a.
15 F. Scott Fitzgerald, "The Crack-Up," *Esquire Magazine*, February, March and April 1936), www.esquire.com/lifestyle/a4310/the-crack-up/.
16 Gilles Deleuze, *Logique du sens* (Paris: Minuit, 1975), pp. 180–1.

17 Ibid., p. 188. Suffering from a serious respiratory illness, Gilles Deleuze committed suicide by jumping out of a window on 4 November 1995, at the age of seventy.

Chapter 5 Desire Late in Life

1 Junichirō Tanizaki, *Journal d'un vieux fou* (Paris: Gallimard, 1962), p. 28.
2 Ibid., p. 63.
3 Ibid., p. 68.
4 Several thousand dollars in today's money.
5 Tennessee Williams, *The Roman Spring of Mrs Stone* (London: Vintage, [1950] 1999). Adapted as a film in 1961 and again in 2003.
6 See the films by Ulrich Seidl, *Paradis: amour* (2014), and Laurent Cantet, *Vers le sud* (2005).
7 Jane Somers [Doris Lessing], *Diary of a Good Neighbor* (New York: Knopf, 1983).
8 Annie Ernaux, *Journal du dehors* (Paris: Gallimard, 1993), p. 101; quoted in Martine Boyer-Weinmann, *Vieillir, dit-elle* (Seyssel: Champ Vallon, 2013), p. 88.
9 Monique Canto-Sperber, "Le Sexe et la vie d'une femme," *Esprit*, no. 273 (March–April 2001), pp. 270–81.
10 Suzanne Kadar, *Elles sont jeunes... eux pas* (Paris: Éditions du Sentier, 2005).
11 Ibid., p. 90.
12 Lisa Halliday, *Asymmetry* (New York: Simon & Schuster, 2018). The novel recounts with humor and distance the affair between the young Alice, twenty-three, and a famous writer, Ezra Blazer, who might be her grandfather; he is seventy-three and is expecting, any year now, a Nobel Prize. Their erotic encounters are sketched out with modesty: Alice slips under the sheets until her old lover "comes like a little water fountain." The man has back trouble, has stents put in, and is constantly on the brink of falling apart, but he is ironic about his physical decline. She worries about him

at the slightest alarm. Ezra Blazer is supposed to be a very indulgent portrait of Philip Roth, with whom Lisa Halliday had an affair when she was young, and to whom the book offers an exaggerated homage.

13 Dominique Simmonet, Joël de Rosnay, François de Closets and Jean-Louis Servan-Schreiber, *Une vie en plus* (Paris: Seuil, 2005), pp. 122–3.

14 This is shown very well in Ulrich Seidl's film *Paradis: amour*, or Laurent Cantet's *Vers le sud*, with Charlotte Rampling (adapted from the book by Dany Laferrière). Middle-aged women leave for countries of the South, the Maghreb, the Caribbean, Haiti, sub-Saharan Africa, Greece or southern Italy: they want well-hung men who will look at them soulfully and embrace them tenderly. The men see in these women simply a source of income and do not fail to hold out their hands as soon as love is consummated. The women are torn between tenderness and sensuality and, while they remunerate their lovers, they would like to be loved for themselves. For example, in the first film, set in Kenya, the main heroine asks the waiter in the hotel to perform cunnilingus on her. He politely refuses, very embarrassed by this request. She weeps. The tragedy is the same for men of the same age captivated by young persons, men or women. The lovers constantly flee or deceive these hoary protectors who pay them and of whom they are ashamed. The journalist and columnist Matthieu Galey recounts how, at the premiere of a play by Bob Wilson in 1978, Louis Aragon flaunted himself in the theatre's dress circle alongside Renaud Camus, who strutted about, billing and cooing. When the old poet fell asleep, Camus elbowed him furiously, with no result, and shot knowing glances to the company at large that seemed to say: "You have to put up with him, the old queen!" Galey, *Journal, 1974–1986* (Paris: Grasset, 1989), pp. 69–70.

15 See François-Xavier Albouy, *Le Prix d'un homme* (Paris: Grasset, 2016), and Denis Kessler, "Quelle est la valeur économique de la vie humaine?" in Roger-Pol Droit (ed.), *Comment penser l'argent?* (Paris: Le Monde, 1992), pp. 310ff.

16 Jean-Marc Jancovici, "L'Europe est en décroissance énergétique depuis 2007," *Socialter*, 12 July 2019.

17 Juliette Noureddine and Alexandre Tharaud, "J'ai pas su y faire" (Maurice Yvain), *Le Boeuf sur le toit*, Virgin Classics, 2012.

18 Freud, letter to Wilhelm Fliess: "Someone who proposes to free humanity from its exuberant sexual subjection, whatever stupidity he chooses to say, will be considered a hero." In the same spirit, this quotation taken from Maïa Mazaurette, "Sexualité des personnes âgées: le grand tabou," *Le Monde*, 29 January 2017: "One expects from old persons a form of the renunciation of earthly pleasures, through a wisdom that is supposed to magically place them beyond the reach of strong emotions .... If we want to believe that old people don't sleep together, that is because we would like to be freed from sex."

19 Seneca, *De beneficiis*.

20 Arthur C. Clarke, *Courrier International*, 16 December 1993, quoted in David Le Breton, *L'Adieu au corps* (Paris: Métaillé, 2013), p. 181.

21 Cicero, *De senectute*.

22 As Gabriel Matzneff mischievously points out in *Le Taureau de Phalaris* (Paris: La Table Ronde, 1987), quoted in René Schérer, "Vieillards d'harmonie," *Le Portique*, no. 21 (2008), https://journals.openedition.org/leportique/1733.

23 Arthur Schnitzler, *Casanova's Homecoming*, trans. Eden Paul and Cedar Paul (Fairfield, IA: 1st World Library, 2006).

Chapter 6 Eros and Agape in the Shadow of Thanatos

1 Heinrich Mann, *Professor Unrat* (1905), trans. Ernest Boyd as *Small Town Tyrant* (New York: Creative Age Press, 1944).

2 *Harold and Maude* (1971), a film directed by Hal Ashby with a screenplay by Colin Higgins and music by Cat Stevens. In

some countries, the film was prohibited for viewers under eighteen years of age.

3 Directed by Robert Mulligan, with a screenplay by Herman Raucher and the very beautiful music of Michel Legrand (1971).

4 In Japan, there are even senior porno actors, such as Shigeo Tokuda, eighty-five years old, a former tourist guide who, at the age of sixty, began a career as an actor in X-rated films. Short, bald, without any particular attraction, he resembles all Japanese retirees; he connects with an audience that shares his condition, and he has made more than 350 videos. This hard-core grandfather, who eats vegetables and eggs, has launched the genre of *old men's porn* in Asia. The porno industry that has popularized MILFs ("Moms I'd like to fuck") – mothers who were already present in the TV series *Desperate Housewives* – also shows "sexy grannies," lustful old ladies, in cute scenarios. This is a small marketing niche that is placed wholly under the sign of the "angel of the bizarre" (Edgar Allan Poe).

5 See the Canadian film *Gerontophilia* (2014), directed by Bruce LaBruce, the story of Lake, a young man of eighteen who lives with his girlfriend and who falls in love with a patient in the retirement home where he works. Mr Peabody, a sick octogenarian, leads him into a passionate and complicit relationship.

6 In her book *Sex & Sixty*, trans. Kate Bignold and Luisa Nitrato Izzo (Melbourne: Scribe, 2016), Marie de Hennezel discusses the case of a resident of a retirement home who is nearly ninety-nine years old and to whom the staff gives a sex toy to help her avoid injuring herself when she masturbates, scandalizing her nephew (p. 196). The author emphasizes the difficulty the caregivers and the family have in understanding the residents' need for bodily closeness and intimacy (pp. 192–4).

7 Romain Gary, *Au-delà de cette limite, votre ticket n'est plus valable* (Paris: Gallimard, 1975). Listening to the confidences of an American businessman who is convinced that

his penis is shrinking and no longer fills the vaginal cavity of his partners, the narrator, a 59-year-old industrialist, is overcome in turn by the fear of impotence, which leads him to destroy his relationship with a young Brazilian woman, Laura. The startling crudeness of this text is also a good example of harmful mimicry.

8 The studies contradict one another, depending on whether sexuality is viewed as coital activity with penetration or as an exchange of caresses or kisses. In one case, contentment is aleatory and, in other, more satisfying (see de Hennezel, *Sex & Sixty*, pp. 170–1).

9 André Gorz, *Lettre à D.* (Paris: Galilée, 2006).

Chapter 7 No More, Too Late, Still!

1 George Steiner, *Errata: An Examined Life* (New Haven, CT: Yale University Press, 1998), p. 175.

2 Brassaï, *Marcel Proust sous l'emprise de la photographie* (Paris: Gallimard, 1997), p. 38.

3 Kohl boasted of having thus escaped Nazi indoctrination. In reality, as his adversaries emphasized, he was born in 1933 and had spent his whole childhood in Hitlerian institutions; in this domain, his innocence was anything but assured.

4 A film directed by Robert Zemeckis (1985), with Michael J. Fox and Christopher Lloyd.

5 This poem was translated by both Charles Baudelaire and Stéphane Mallarmé.

6 Simone de Beauvoir, *The Force of Circumstance*, trans. Richard Howard, in *Hard Times: The Force of Circumstance*, vol. 2: *1952–1962* (New York: Da Capo Press, 1994), p. 379.

7 Italo Svevo, *Zeno's Conscience*, trans. William Weaver (New York: Vintage, 2003), pp. 13–14.

8 Thomas Jefferson, letter to William Stephens Smith, 13 November 1787, concerning Shay's Rebellion in Massachusetts; for a photocopy of the original, see www. snopes.com/fact-check/thomas-jefferson-tree-of-liberty/.

9 Gustave Flaubert, *Sentimental Education*, trans. Helen Constantine (Oxford: Oxford University Press, 2016), p. 388.

10 *Le Livre des morts égyptien*, quoted by Jean Vermette, *La Réincarnation* (Paris: Que sais-je?, 1995).

11 Plato, *The Republic*, 617e–619a.

12 Marcel Proust, *In Search of Lost Time*, Vol. 3: *The Guermantes Way*, trans. C. K. Scott-Moncrieff (New Haven, CT: Yale University Press, 2018).

13 Jean-Yves Tadié, *Proust et le roman* (Paris: Gallimard, 1986), p. 331.

14 Philip José Farmer, *To Your Scattered Bodies Go* (New York: Berkley, 1971). I read this novel in 1989.

15 At the resurrection, the body will indeed be identical with the earthly body, but freed of weight, of its "tunic of skin," and returned to its resemblance to God. On Gregory of Nyssa's opposition to Origen, see Bernard Pottier, "L'humanité du Christ selon Grégoire de Nysse," *Nouvelle Revue de Théologie*, no. 120 (1998), pp. 353–69.

Chapter 8 Make a Success of One's Life, and Then What?

1 See Dorian Astor, *Deviens ce que tu es: pour une vie philosophique* (Paris: Autrement, 2016).

2 Charles Péguy, in *Cahiers de la Quinzaine*, 12 and 23 October 1910, quoted by Michel Philibert, *L'Échelle des âges* (Paris: Seuil, 1968), pp. 217–18.

3 "Since I undertook the study of the unconscious, I seem very interesting to myself." Sigmund Freud, letter to Wilhelm Fliess, 3 December 1897.

4 Jean-Paul Sartre, *The Words*, trans. Bernard Frechtman (New York: Vintage, 1981), p. 242. On this subject, see Olivier Rey's excellent commentary in *Une folle solitude* (Paris: Seuil, 2006), pp. 244–5.

5 Michel Foucault, *Philosophie* (Paris: Gallimard, 2004), p. 62.

6 Rainer Maria Rilke, *The Notebooks of Malte Laurids Brigge* (Oxford: Oxford University Press, 2016), p. 6.
7 Georges Bernanos, *Diary of a Country Priest*, trans. Pamela Morris (Boston: Da Capo, 2002), p. 109.
8 See Luc Ferry's remarkable essay *Qu'est-ce qu'une vie réussie?* (Paris: Grasset, 2002).
9 In 2009–10, the Museum of Modern Art in Paris organized an exhibit called "Deadline," on the latest works of twelve internationally known artists on the threshold of death. Among them were paintings by De Kooning, Hans Hartung and Chen Zhen, along with Robert Mapplethorpe's photographs of busts and skulls.
10 Stefan Zweig, *Schachnovelle* (Frankfurt am Main: Fischer, [1942] 2009).
11 Constantine Cavafy, "Ithaka," in *Collected Poems*, trans. Edmund Keeley and Philip Sherrard (rev. edn, Princeton, NJ: Princeton University Press, 1992), pp. 37–8. Vladimir Jankélévitch imagines a modern Odysseus as a prodigal son who gets bored, once he has returned to his Penelope, and dreams again about Calypso in her seaside grotto, as well as about Circé, because he has traded nostalgia for disappointment. See Jankélévitch, *L'Irréversible et la nostalgie* (Paris: Flammarion, 1983), pp. 291–2.
12 In Éric Deschavanne and Pierre-Henri Tavoillot, *Philosophie des âges de la vie* (Paris: Grasset, 2007), pp. 305–6.
13 Marcel Proust, *In Search of Lost Time*, Vol. 2: *In the Shadow of Young Girls in Flower*, trans. C. K. Scott-Moncrieff (New Haven, CT: Yale University Press, 2015), p. 254.
14 On the notion of a second life, see Jankélévitch (*L'Irréversible et la nostalgie*, pp. 75–7), who notes that Lazarus' new life after he is raised from the tomb resembles the recapitulation of a sonata. On the same subject, but in a rhetoric close to Heidegger and influenced by Chinese thought, see François Jullien, *Une seconde vie* (Paris: Grasset, 2016).
15 Nicholas Negroponte, *Being Digital* (New York: Vintage, 1995).
16 See Catherine Chalier, *Transmettre de génération en génération* (Paris: Buchet-Chastel, 2008), pp. 230–1.

17 Marc Lambron, *Vie et mort de Michael Jackson* (Paris: Réunion des musées nationaux, 2018), p. 29.

Chapter 9 Death, Where is Thy Victory?

1 Guy de Maupassant, *Bel Ami* (Paris: Paul Ollendorf, 1901), p. 160.
2 André Klarsfeld and Frédéric Revah, *Biologie de la mort* (Paris: Odile Jacob, 2000). According to these authors, no superior law condemns beings to ageing and death.
3 Jean-Claude Ameisen, *La Sculpture du vivant* (Paris: Seuil, 2003). According to the author, repressing the triggering of cellular suicide and thus prolonging life beyond the accepted limits has become the fascinating goal of medicine in the twenty-first century.
4 Marcel Proust, *In Search of Lost Time*, Vol. 2: *In the Shadow of Young Girls in Flower*, trans. C. K. Scott-Moncrieff (New Haven, CT: Yale University Press, 2015).
5 Jean-Michel Besnier, *Demain les posthumains: le futur a-t-il encore besoin de nous?* (Paris: Hachette Pluriel, 2009).
6 In 2014, on the website capital.fr. See also "L'homme qui vivra mille ans est déjà né," an interview that appeared on 30 July of the same year. In his book published in 2011, Dr Alexandre announced in a messianic tone "la mort de la mort" (The death of death, Paris: J. C. Lattès). According to him, it would no longer be a reality imposed by nature or by a god but a problem to be solved. In the course of the twenty-first century, he said, we would pass, thanks to the "geno-tsunami," from man repaired to man augmented, who would be potentially immortal.
7 See www.orlan.eu/petition/.
8 Julie de la Brosse, "Démiurges et milliardaires," *L'Express*, 10 August 2017.
9 St Augustine, *Confessions*, Book 10, chap. 40.
10 The Greeks subdivided immortality into three parts: the crudest, sexual reproduction; the most heroic, the warrior's

glory; and the only authentic immortality, for both Plato and Aristotle, the contemplation of wisdom.

11 Quoted in Vladimir Jankélévitch, *L'Irréversible et la nostalgie* (Paris: Flammarion, 1983), pp. 68–9.
12 Alfred de Vigny, "La Maison du berger," in *Les Destinées* (Paris: Pichon, 1930).
13 Jacques Prévert, "Le jardin," in *Paroles* (Paris: Le Point du Jour, 1946).
14 Alfred de Musset, "Souvenir," in *Revue des Deux Mondes* (1841).
15 See Lucian Boia's excellent book *Quant les centenaires seront jeunes* (Paris: Les Belles Lettres, 2006).
16 Quoted in Jean-François Braunstein, "Auguste Comte, la Vierge Mère et les vaches folles: les utopies biomédicales du positivisme," in Lucien Sfez (ed.), *L'Utopie de la santé parfaite: colloque de Cerisy* (Paris: PUF, 2001), pp. 289–99.
17 Cicero, *De senectute*.
18 *Night of the Living Dead* (1968).
19 Maxime Coulombe, *Petite philosophie du zombie* (Paris: PUF, 2012), p. 71. See also Nicole Lafontaine, *La Société postmortelle* (Paris: Seuil, 2008), pp. 86–7, on the new frontiers of research on brain death and the transformation of death into an administrative decision. The brain is now seen as the nucleus of the individual. The dying person intubated and hooked up to machines is the true cyborg of today (pp. 83–5).

Chapter 10 The Immortality of Mortals

1 Gabriel García Márquez, *Memories of My Melancholy Whores*, trans. Edith Grossman (New York: Knopf, 2005).
2 François-René de Chateaubriand, *Mémoires d'outre-tombe* (Paris: Garnier Flammarion, 1982), p. 359.
3 Such as Boethius, *The Consolation of Philosophy* (the diary of a prisoner condemned to death, written by this sixth-century Latin poet). See Marc Fumaroli's introduction to

a French translation (Paris: Rivages, [1989] 2020). English edition, trans. Richard H. Green (Oxford: Blackwell, 2003).

4 For example, Seneca's *Of Consolation: To Marcia*, trans. Aubrey Stewart (London: George Bell, 1900), https://en.wikisource.org/wiki/Of_Consolation:_To_Marcia.

5 Marcus Aurelius, *Meditations*.

6 Seneca, *Ad Lucilium epistulae morales*, trans. Richard M. Gummere (London: Heineman, 1917), vol. 1, letter 12, p. 9.

7 Epictetus, *The Enchiridion, or Manual*, trans. George Long (New York: Dover, 2004), §VIII.

8 "The dreadful, terrible act of his dying, he saw, was reduced by all those around him to the level of an accidental unpleasantness, partly an indecency (something like dealing with a man who comes into a drawing room spreading a bad smell)." *The Death of Ivan Ilyich and Other Stories*, trans. Richard Pevear (New York: Vintage, 2010), p. 75.

9 Sigmund Freud, "Thoughts for the Times on War and Death" (1915), in *The Standard Edition of the Complete Psychological Works*, ed. and trans. James Strachey et al., vol. 14 (London: Hogarth Press, 1971).

10 St Augustine, *The City of God*.

11 Bertrand Vergely, *La Souffrance* (Paris: Gallimard, 1997), p. 306. And again: "To die after living is not to die altogether. For anyone who has lived, lives on, and will live forever, finding in the presence of this rich past of life the very presence that allows him to transcend death" (p. 260).

12 Epicurus, *Letter to Menoeceus*, trans. Robert Drew Hicks, http://classics.mit.edu/Epicurus/menoec.html.

13 Bossuet, *Sermon sur la mort* (Paris: Seuil, 1997), p. 201.

14 Fénelon, *Livre de prières avec ses Réflexions saintes pour tous les jours du mois*, 27e jour.

15 Paul Veyne, *Sénèque* (Paris: Texto, 2007), preface by Louis Jerphagnon.

16 Seneca, *Of Consolation*, §XXIII.

17 Ibid., §XXII.

18 Ibid., §XXV.